MILITARY MARCHING
A Pictorial History

Dedicated to the memory of my son
Ian James Cramer, formerly of the
17th/21st Lancers, who was tragically
killed at Robertsbridge, East Sussex
in 1988

© James Cramer, 1992

First published in the UK in
1992 by
SPELLMOUNT LTD
12 Dene Way
Speldhurst
Tunbridge Wells
Kent
TN3 0NX

British Library Cataloguing in
Publication Data
Military marching: Pictorial History
- (Military Pictorial History).
1 Armies, History. I. Title. II. Series
356.109
ISBN 0-946771-79-0

Printed in Great Britain
by
BIDDLES LTD
Woodbridge Park
Guildford
Surrey

Published works by the same author:

THE WORLD'S POLICE
UNIFORMS OF THE WORLD'S POLICE
POLICE ANIMALS OF THE WORLD
A HISTORY OF THE POLICE OF PORTSMOUTH
THE BOOK OF PORTSMOUTH
DEATH ON THE COMMON: THE TRIAL AND EXECUTION OF
DAVID TYRIE, TRAITOR, AT PORTSMOUTH 1782

MILITARY
MARCHING

A PICTORIAL HISTORY

James Cramer

Foreword by
Lt-Gen Sir Napier Crookenden, KCB, DSO, OBE, DL

SPELLMOUNT LTD
Tunbridge Wells

CONTENTS

Acknowledgements

I am immensely grateful to many people and organisations for their help in collating material in connection with this work.

In particular I thank naval, military and air force authorities in Great Britain and overseas, government departments, embassies, libraries, museums, newspapers, magazines and arms manufacturers, to name but a few of the sources I have consulted.

On a personal note I value the help of my friends Dr Klaus-Ulrich Keubke, a military historian, and his wife Erna, a distinguished military artist, both of Potsdam; Richard Ostler and Jill Du Bois for their help in the compilation and recording of historical material; artists David Russell and Douglas Coyne; John Sellars, an outstanding military artist and painter; Bernard Collins, Cliff Dredge and Ron Harris for supplying rare photographs and pictures of marching infantry; Edward Ryan, Divisional Bibliographical Librarian of Portsmouth Central Library, who allowed me to study many books of the nineteenth and early twentieth centuries in the book store, providing valuable illustrative material for this work.

The curators of regimental museums have been very kind to me, particularly those of the Royal Green Jackets Museum and Light Infantry Museum who went out of their way to find exciting material in their archives.

I wish to thank the publishers of military books and news agencies who have helped to provide material for this book, in particular Associated Book Publishers (UK) Limited (*From Sepoy to Subedar* by James Lunt); A & C Black (*The Roman Soldier* by Amédée Forestier); Xinhua News Agency (for photographs of the Chinese People's Army); Imperial War Museum, Victoria and Albert Museum and British Museum: DDR Museum, Dresden; Random Century Group (for *Rank and File* edited by T.H. McGuffie); the Albion Press Limited (for *Gone for a Soldier* by Victor Neuberg); Macdonald & Co. (Publishers) Ltd (for extract from *Nam* by Mark Baker) and apologise most profoundly for any omissions to the list.

Finally, my grateful thanks are due to Captain and Adjutant N.C. Hearn, Welsh Guards and Regimental Sergeant Major Andrew Phasey BEM of the Grenadier Guards for enabling me to visit the Guards Depot, Pirbright and see for myself that the standards of drill and marching are still as high as they were in 1939 when I absorbed the benefits of the Guards recruits' training.

As a result of all my research I have come to the conclusion, belatedly, that my first drill instructor was right when he told our recruit squad that 'There's more to marching than putting one bleeding foot before the other!'

*   *   *   *

AUTHOR'S NOTE

Since the completion of this book the world has seen the break-up not only of the Soviet Union but also the Warsaw Pact and as such all references to their armies must be treated in the spirit of the times when the book was written.

Now, to turn to marching matters:-
I've my knapsack, firelock, spatters,
Crossbelts, priming-horn, stock, bay'net, blackball, clay,
Pouch, magazine, and flint-box that at every quickstep clatters;
My heart, Dear; that must stay.

Thomas Hardy, 'The Alarm'.

Troops who march in an irregular and disorderly manner are always in great danger of being defeated.

Vegetius: 'De Re Militari.' AD 378.

An Army without Rule a Tumult is.

Lieutenant Colonel Richard Eaton:
'The Compleat Body of the Art Military.' 1659.

A third-class ride's better than a first-class walk!

An old British infantry adage.

FOREWORD

by Lt-Gen Sir Napier Crookenden, KCB, DSO, OBE, DL

James Cramer takes me back to 1935, when I joined the 2nd Battalion, The Cheshire Regiment, at Catterick in Yorkshire and to those happy, far off days, when we moved everywhere on our feet and our gear followed us in horse drawn wagons or on the backs of mules. Taught to march by Grenadier Guards, the author learned in the Royal Northumberland Fusiliers to 'long carry' the 40-odd pounds weight of a Vickers machine gun or its tripod and marched across France, Belgium, Holland and Germany with the 1st Battalion, the Royal Ulster Rifles.

In the years between the wars British infantry marched everywhere, to their meals, to their training, to the ranges, or to their next station and to move by motor transport or by train was exceptional. We wore our boots continuously, each and every day and the 'care of the feet' was instilled into every officer and NCO. Every week, usually on Saturdays, we did a battalion route march of 10 to 15 miles and the ability to march long distances was taken for granted.

Most of this went by the board as the Army became mechanised. In World War II infantry still went into battle on their feet, but most strategic moves were made in motor transport. Certainly the Fourteenth Army slogged on their feet through the jungle for months at a time and in North West Europe the parachute and glider battalions of Airborne Forces, knowing that they would have no transport on landing other than jeeps, made a fetish of long marches as a way of achieving the physical hardness on which their survival depended.

James Cramer and I served in the 6th Airlanding Brigade of the 6th Airborne Division, he in the Royal Ulster Rifles - six hundred or so cheerful Irishmen, with a leavening of Sassenach volunteers, most of them Regular soldiers - and myself as Brigade Major. We were lucky in having a year in which to prepare for D-Day and I have a vivid memory of the long columns of the brigade, marching back to Bulford from all over the South of

England at the end of one of our frequent exercises. It was a point of honour for each battalion to complete the journey in good time without stragglers and for us in the rag, tag and bobtail of Brigade Headquarters to spurn our jeeps and reach barracks as fast, if not faster than the battalions.

The 6th Airborne Division certainly learned in Germany the value of their previous march training, for after the Rhine Crossing we marched on our feet almost the whole way to the Baltic, as James Cramer relates.

British and American infantry may have ridden into battle in armoured carriers during the Gulf War, but only nine years before the Falklands Campaign showed that the foot soldier must still learn to march long distances and to look after his feet!

This is a fascinating and comprehensive study, in which everyone interested in military marching or, for that matter civilian walking, will find much pleasure and a lot to learn. James does well to remind us of Marshal Saxe's words "in the legs lies all the secret of manoeuvres and combats."

Preface

Before discussing the development of military marching through the ages it is necessary, in the first instance, to establish what exactly is understood by the term *marching*. Under the heading 'March' most dictionaries describe the movement as a 'walk in a military manner with regular and measured tread' or 'to walk in step, to go forward with a regular and uniform movement.' The word 'march' in the military sense is apparently derived from the Old French *marcher* 'to walk', originally 'to tread or trample', which in turn came from the Gallo-Roman *marcare* ('to beat') from the Late Latin *marcus* 'a hammer'. Other etymological sources describe a march as 'a movement together on foot and in time, as of soldiers; a stately and dignified walk with a rhythmic stride and in step with others; to move in a direct and purposeful manner, in an organised column' and so on. (The word 'march' seems to have been used first in relation to walking in a military manner circa 1515).

Armed only with this information it might appear that military forces can only be described as 'marching' when every soldier in a column is walking in step with the rest of the body 'in a stately and dignified manner'. The early use of the Latin words for 'to beat' and 'hammer' reinforces the notion of the regular beat of nailed boots on a hard road surface and the regular heavy tramp of a host on the march.

If the definitions of 'marching' set out above were to be the only criteria it is plain that some of the greatest or most historic marches would have to be re-named. The men who marched over the Alps with Hannibal in 218 BC or who suffered during Marlborough's famed march to the Danube in 1704 or who endured the Chinese Communists' remarkable Long March of 1934-35 certainly did not, by all accounts, walk in a stately, dignified manner nor did they move with measured, regular strides in step with their comrades for very long; their energies were directed towards coping with the difficulties of the terrain they were traversing and their own exhaustion, let alone the constant threat of attack or ambush and the fighting of savage pitched battles with opposing forces. Any soldier who has struggled across muddy, ploughed fields in a rainstorm or pushed his way through a cornfield under a blazing sun, while heavily and awkwardly laden with arms and equipment, knows full well that cadenced marching or walking in step with his comrades for any length of time in these circumstances is well nigh impossible and unnecessary.

For the purpose of the present work, therefore, the term *marching* is taken to mean the movement of military bodies in a generally disciplined and orderly manner.

Artist's impression of Roman 'tortoise' (testudo) manoeuvre used against walls or ramparts (27-man group)

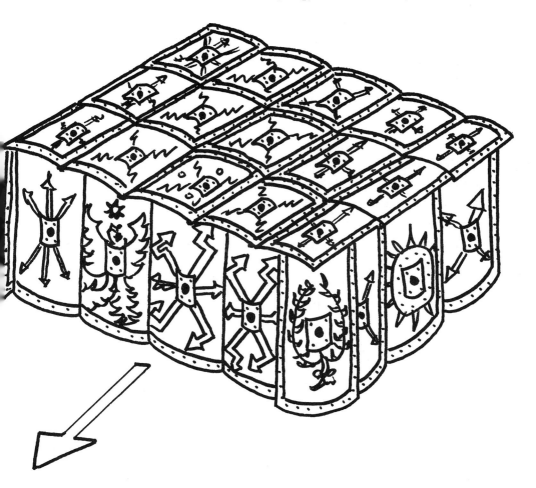

Chapter One

The Origins of the Foot Soldier and Military Marching

The origins of soldiers and armies cannot be dated but prehistoric artifacts and cave drawings confirm that our ancestors fought on foot with sticks and wooden clubs and, probably, with heavy stones, in the course of disputes with neighbouring tribes over hunting rights, border disputes or acquisition of the property of others.

The establishment of city states in Mesopotamia and Egypt and their continual struggle for the possession of arable lands and water rights, disputes over boundaries and the later expansion into kingdoms and empires must have accentuated the development of armies from the bands of warriors already set up in those areas.

The Sumerians provide the first historical evidence of any army organisation; this is in the third millennium BC. The so-called 'Standard', discovered in one of the royal graves of Ur, depicts foot soldiers armed with short spears, wearing copper helmets and protected by thick reinforced cloaks, all, apparently, walking in step. Later, the Sumerian army tactical formations were standardised on a six-man deep phalanx; the first ranks went into combat carrying large rectangular shields and the rest of the host bore heavy pikes and battle axes. Although the soldiers shown in the 'Standard' mosaic appear to be marching in step, this did not necessarily mean that they did so in reality. Many ancient artifacts depicting warriors on the move, marching in step in perfect alignment, may have been designed in this fashion because the artist or sculptor wanted to achieve a neat, symmetrical pattern in his work. Examples of this kind of work appear in battle scenes drawn and sculpted many centuries later - the most striking being a contemporary picture of the sixteenth century Spanish conquistador, Hernan Cortes, who overthrew the Aztec Empire (1519-21) and won Mexico for the crown of Spain. His soldiers, native porters and their women and even the forelegs of the commander's horse are all in perfect step, with their left feet leading.

Although no other evidence has yet been found that the troops of Sumeria marched in step there is a probability that when the men were deployed in phalanx formation they might have found it more convenient to do so. When the phalanx was being formed the men in the front rank were often required to bear, on their shoulders, the weight of the heavy pikes of their comrades in the rearmost ranks, besides struggling to control their own pikes. If the troops were *not* marching in step the shafts of the pikes would have jarred and bumped painfully on the shoulders of the men in front.

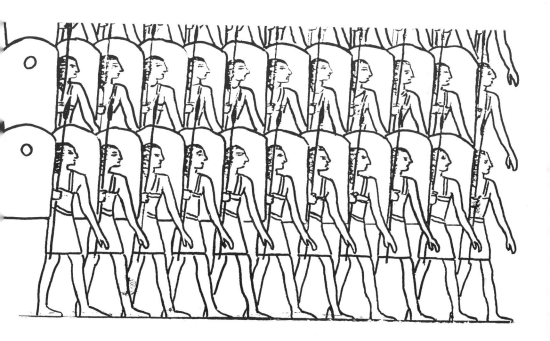

Part of an Egyptian phalanx circa 2000 AD

Under Rameses II (who reigned from 1292 to 1225 BC) the Egyptian army reached its ultimate state of organisation. The foot soldiers wore comparatively light clothing of laminated cloth as armour and leather caps. The tactical formations were based on a square of one hundred men deep. Recruit training courses were set up and wings, centre and flanking formations were practised. In these manoeuvres, of necessity, to prevent confusion when deploying before battle was joined, a cadenced step was introduced whereby a rhythmic measured stride was maintained and uniformity of movement assured. To help the troops to keep step musicians with flutes accompanied the units on the march.

At the time of the Trojan War (about 1180 BC) Greek foot soldiers are portrayed in classical pictures wearing bronze helmets with visors and a projection at the back to protect the neck, and a crest with a plume or long mane. Body armour generally consisted of a jerkin of leather of strips of strengthened material. The shield was long, often covering the soldier from head to foot. Greaves protected the legs below the knees and were made of bands of cloth or leather secured with buckles. Leather sandals were worn. Weapons included spears and a short sword or dagger.

Representation of Mycenaean warriors from 12th century BC 'Warrior Vase', carrying crescent-shaped pelta shields and wearing bronze helmets, supposed to be from the Trojan War period.

The weight of the weapons and shield, together with the type of defensive clothing worn, must have caused extreme discomfort when negotiating difficult ground. Nowhere was this more obvious than during the retreat of the Greeks after the battle of Cunaxa in 401 BC. Wearing clothing and carrying arms similar to that described above, but with the addition of bronze breastplates and metal greaves, the 12,000 men marched from the Euphrates to the Black Sea, a distance said to be between 600 and a thousand miles. They moved over the mountains of Armenia in appalling winter winds and snow, suffering greatly from attacks from the Persians and barbarian hill peoples. Their ordeal lasted five months and at the end only about 6,000 men survived.

Before the time of Alexander the Great (4th century BC) many armies marched and manoeuvred to the sound of the flute, particularly when dusk or mist obscured visual signals. Later the flute was replaced by the trumpet which could more easily be heard over the sounds of battle.

In Thucydides' account of the battle of Mantinea in 418 BC between the Spartans and their allies and the Argives and theirs he described how the latter advanced with undisciplined haste and fury and the former slowly, with dignity and precision and to the music of many flute players. The Spartans had found that advancing slowly, in step, preserved their formation for the moment of engaging - rather than dissolving in confusion, as large armies were wont to do under these circumstances.

In the summer of 1974 one of the greatest archaeological discoveries in the world was found in a north-western province of China. An army of terra cotta warriors, in life-size proportions, was drawn up in ruler-straight ranks, each standing stiffly to attention. They wore a standardised military uniform. The figures, about 6,000 discovered to date, had been made to stand guard over the tomb of China's first emperor - Qin Shi Huangdi - who died in 210 BC. The foot soldiers' formation shows the pattern which military commanders sought to impose upon their troops during that period - a system which was to be repeated many centuries later on battlefields thousands of miles away to the west.

Artist's impression of a Greek phalanx advancing

From ancient times the phalanx was considered to be the natural tactical formation suitable for members of military citizen armies, whose training and use of tactical movements had to be of the simplest nature. Battle in the early days nearly always took place on a level ground and, ideally, in narrow valleys where the only manoeuvre necessary was a forward or backward movement to drive the enemy from his position or force him back into his city or village whence he came.

Although the system of drill required to form a phalanx and manoeuvre with it was designed to be suitable for a civilian soldier it seems to have required a good deal of training. Young soldiers were first taught to march in single file and when they had mastered this they were instructed how to form up in columns of various depths. If an enemy appeared in the rear of the phalanx each file of soldiers had to be counter-marched, a complex and dangerous manoeuvre on the battlefield. Later, long pikes, some about 21 feet (6.40 metres) long, were used so that men in the rear ranks were able to insert their pikes between the front-line men, in some cases resting upon their shoulders. Round shields, held across the chest, covered a warrior from chin to knees. When the phalanx was drawn up in close order, the shield was wide enough to protect the unguarded side of the man on the warrior's left. All these requirements could best be met by the men taking up precise positions in the formation and keeping in step whilst carrying out the various evolutions of the phalanx.

Besides what was required of him when carrying out the ever-increasing number of battlefield evolutions the soldier also had to endure the ordeal of lengthy or forced marches. In the spring of 218 BC Hannibal set out from Carthagena at the head of 90,000 foot and 12,000 horse and 37 war elephants. After engagements in Spain and Gaul the army took fifteen days to cross over the Alps and into Italy. By the time the expedition was over the Carthagenians had marched 962 miles in a period of five months and had lost three-quarters of their army - with not more than 20,000 foot soldiers and 6,000 cavalrymen surviving.

For six centuries the Roman legions were the supreme foot soldiers. They appear, moreover, to have been laden with an extraordinary amount of equipment - alarmingly large according to some authorities. Cicero wrote of 'the toil, the great toil of the march: the load of more than half a month's provisions, the load of any and everything that might be required, the load of the stake for entrenchments.'

The Roman soldier carried a pick-axe, tent, stakes, semi-circular long shield, spare thongs, cloak, personal kit for washing and shaving, rations, a length of rope; a chain, saw and hook, kept in a toolbag and a wicker basket for moving earth; a bronze food box or mess tin, a kettle and, perhaps a portable hand mill for grinding corn. He wore a metal helmet with cheek and chin guards, a corselet of circular iron bands, hinged behind and fastened with a clasp over the chest, with shoulder pieces over a woollen tunic. His personal weapons included a short sword and javelin. Sandals extended a short way up the leg. These were an important part of the soldier's clothing. They were, in many ways, as serviceable and tough as the modern army boot. The soles, made of several layers of leather and heavily studded with heavy-beaded

Heavily laden Roman legionary circa 120-100 BC

iron or bronze nails, varied considerably in thickness - perhaps three-quarters of an inch (1.91 cm) was the average. Strips of cloth or fur were sometimes inserted inside the sandals for comfort. Sandals were secured to the foot and ankle by leather thongs.

An individual load carried by a legionary sometimes amounted to 100 lbs (45.36 kg) and he was appositely nicknamed 'Marius's Mule' because of the amount of armour, equipment, weapons and supplies he carried on the march. The name was taken from Gaius Marius (155-86 BC), the general who laid the foundations for a well-disciplined Roman army.

For the Romans marching constituted the principal part of the soldier's training. The first thing taught was the military step, so as to accustom the troops to march quickly and together. It was laid down that they should march with the common military step twenty miles[1] in five summer hours and with the full step, which was quicker, 24 miles in the same number of hours. When that pace was exceeded, the men no longer marched but ran, in which case no certain rate could be assigned. The recruits were constantly exercised in running in order to be able to charge the enemy with great vigour, to occupy an advantageous position speedily so as to anticipate the arrival of an enemy there, to reconnoitre quickly and get back rapidly, to follow a retreating enemy and to overtake him in pursuit.

The Roman armies were noted for their rapid marching. This reputation was maintained up to the 3rd century AD, then the speed and distances covered decreased in a marked manner. This was accounted for, in part, it is said, by the lack of good recruits and in part by the greater amount of baggage taken with them and the weight of the engines of war to be manhandled in their campaigns.

In the Second Punic War against Hannibal the Roman army showed its marching ability under the young Scipio in the seizure of New Carthage. In this brilliant feat speed and surprise were essential. The small army did a rapid march of about 200 miles in six days and arrived at the same time as the Roman fleet, thus successfully attacking the town simultaneously.

From the time of the foundation of the city of Rome the legions first copied the pattern of the solid Greek phalanx but as the territory of Rome grew larger the system became too unwieldy for the hills and valleys of central Italy and the long process of inventing and practising new tactics for the legions began.

---

[1] The Roman mile contained 1617 English yards or 143 yards less than the English statute mile.

Artist's impression of Hannibal's army crossing the Alps 218 BC

At the time of the Punic Wars the legions formed up for battle in what looked like three rows of a chessboard. The fit young soldiers were in the front line (*hastati*), the battle-hardened veterans were in the second line (*principes*) and the oldest men were in the third line (*triarii*). Recruits from 17 to 25 years (*velites*) normally occupied skirmishing positions in front of the *hastati* until driven back by the enemy. They then retreated to occupy the intervals between the columns (maniples) of the *triarii*. When under heavy attack the maniples of the *hastati* could fall back in an orderly fashion into the intervals of the *principes* or, conversely, on the offensive the *principes* could march forward to utilise the intervals between the front-line maniples.

Whether the Roman legions actually marched in step has been a matter of dispute among historians. An ancient work by Claudius Aelianus, in the time of the Emperor Hadrian, is said to give an accurate account of the orders and drill movements of the Roman army of the period, including references to the formation of the 'Orb' and 'Tortoise' (*Testudo*) positions, to resist an attack by cavalry, and a preparation for an attack on a fortified position respectively. Although there does not seem to be any firm evidence that the legions marched in step, it is difficult to imagine the 'Tortoise' formation being completed and operated successfully if the men involved were allowed to pick their own pace time and length of stride. The 'Tortoise' was used to approach walls and ramparts. One example would consist of a body of 27 men formed up in four rows. A front row of six crouched down behind the shields of the middle four men which were held rim to rim. The two end men turned their shields outwards. The second, third and fourth rows of seven men each closed up behind in a similar way but the middle five men in each rank held their shields above their heads. There are stories of chariots being driven across and over these formations to test their strength. It is easy to imagine how insecure the 'walls' and 'ceilings' of the *testudo* would have been if men were out of step, so allowing gaps to appear in the defences and shields to clash against each other or buckle under a heavy weight being applied from above or laterally.

Even in those early days the importance of marching and keeping station was being stressed and Vegetius, the Roman military writer, in his *De Re Militari* of 378 AD, observed that 'troops who march in an irregular and disorderly manner are always in great danger of being defeated.'

A people who seemed to disregard set patterns of warfare at the time were the Huns under their great leader Attila. He had his seat of government in the plains east of the Danube. His rule once stretched from the Rhine into Central Asia. Tacitus described the way in which these Germanic peoples marched and fought on foot. They were arranged in bodies which were as deep as they were wide - in other words the front and rear and both flanks were equally strong: 400 men in a square twenty deep and twenty wide or 10,000 in a formation 100 deep and 100 wide. These squares were as much a feature of the tactics of the Huns as the phalanx had been the original tactical formation of the Greeks and Romans. The square came about because the Huns possessed relatively little protective armour and few metal weapons. They therefore placed their best armed men in the front ranks to protect those not so well armed in the centre of the square. Only a few possessed a spear with a metal head or a sword. Most of the men on foot carried missiles such as stones or stone balls hurled from slings and were usually bare-chested or clad in light clothing which did not hinder their movement. They carried shields made of wood or wickerwork covered with leather. Men wielding the long spear could not carry a shield and it was the practice for men carrying smaller weapons like hand axes to protect them with their shields.

The Huns knew nothing of military discipline and there is no evidence to suggest that their squares ever carried out military exercises. Because of their basic groupings of a hundred families of warriors each man in a square was related to others by ties of blood, thus bringing a cohesion based upon the certainty that each man could rely on those around him in battle. The main strength of the Huns relied on their foot soldiers and because of this they were able to fight in mixed formations of horse and foot in which the men on foot, because of their fitness and dexterity, could adjust to the movements of the cavalry.

A significant battle was fought at Adrianople in 378 AD when cavalry demonstrated an ascendancy over foot soldiers that was to last through the Middle Ages. The peerless Roman legionary of Caesar's day had gradually declined in discipline and patriotic fervour. Mobility was reduced by a greater desire for protection. This took the form, among others, of relying on the *testudo* of overlapping shields in close formation. The Romans became so dependent on this manoeuvre that in battle they could only stand in a mass incapable of manoeuvre while their unsupported lightly-armed foot soldiers and outnumbered horse were cut to pieces around them by the more mobile Gothic cavalry.

From the time of the fall of Rome in 401 AD the shock cavalry tactics of barbarian cavalry bore all before them and the heavily-armed, iron-mailed horsemen replaced the foot soldiers as the dominant force on the battlefields of Europe and the Mediterranean. Over a thousand years were to pass before the foot soldiers, later to be designated 'Infantry', regained their former prestige on the battlefield.

Soldiers in the army of Camillus (circa 396 BC)

Chapter Two

The Decline in Importance of the Foot Soldier and his Re-appearance as an Infantryman; the Emphasis on Cadenced Marching and Drill from the Fifteenth-Century.

During the first centuries after the break-up of the Roman Empire various nations and peoples appeared on the scene and then faded away after initial successes in the field. The Muslims roamed almost unchecked throughout the Mediterranean world. They were hardy soldiers, well disciplined and well led but seemed to rely more upon brute force and numbers than upon newly conceived tactics and drill. The cavalry arm, reserved for followers of Islam, formed the major element of the hosts. The horsemen wore chain-mail and metal helmets and carried swords, bows, daggers and scimitars but relied mainly on their six-foot (1.83 metres) long Arab lances. Eventually, when they realised the value of a strong centre in battle, like that of the legion and phalanx of old, they used European mercenaries for that purpose, on foot.

The Muslims met their match at the battle of Tours in 732 AD when their cavalry could not vanquish the foot soldiers of the Franks and withdrew after six days of manoeuvring. The Muslim threat against Christianity was never again to reach so far into Europe and this was mainly due to the fact that the Franks had retained the old Roman system of well-trained foot soldiers. Few other nations had done likewise - only in England and Denmark had the armed man on foot retained a semblance of his ancient prestige.

Later, however, under the Franks, a system of land-holding and military service developed into what became known as feudalism. The conquerors of a land became the lords; the con-quered, the serfs. Serving the armoured knights on horseback in battle were the poorly-armed and ill-protected serf foot soldiers, trying to fend off the charges of the enemy cavalry and even in danger of being cut down by their own horsed knights if they got in the way of their charge or retreat.

Behind the barrier of the Channel the English retained the old military customs, supplementing their weapons with the huge two-handed axe adopted from the Viking invaders of their shores. The Vikings or Northmen had come from Denmark and Norway, were well-armed warriors, clothed in mail shirts and armed with axes, spears, javelins, bows and arrows and swords. It needs little imagination to understand the fear in the minds of any community at the mercy of the fierce invaders who, after a long row and sail from the Continent, would attack the nearest town or settlement after a series of forced marches on foot or mounted on horses seized from the coastal areas. Then, after an orgy of destruction and slaughter, the invaders would return with their booty to their ships and sail or row away before English reinforcements could be collected and marched to the scene.

The army which Harold marched south from Yorkshire after the battle of Stamford Bridge in 1066 was predominantly a force of men who fought on foot. The nucleus of the army was the personal bodyguard of housecarls, around which were grouped the lighter armed and less well-trained shire levies. The housecarls wore conical steel caps and leather shirts covered with small steel rings, placed close together to withstand sword cuts; their legs were swathed in cloth, held in position by spirally wound leather thongs. They were armed with shields and great axes and many carried light javelins. The shire levies were much less well equipped; for protection most wore a metal cap of sorts but otherwise relied on a stout leather jerkin, while the main personal weapon was the spear, with some having swords or knives.

After the exhausting march, practically the whole length of England, the English were in no condition for an important battle but Harold decided to fight a defensive contest, with few archers and next to no cavalry, with disastrous consequences for himself and his country.

After the Norman Conquest feudalism was introduced in England, with its attendant system of land-holding and military service. The system had one important drawback in that service in the field was limited to forty days a year and the English kings soon realised that feudal levies produced a mob of poorly trained, undisciplined foot soldiers unfit for lengthy campaigning. Later it was deemed desirable to pay wages to fighting men and military service became the acknowledged duty of freemen, the foot soldiers being drawn by county levies.

A flying column of Mongol cavalry

The zenith of cavalry warfare came with the success of the Mongols in the twelfth century, under their leader Genghis Khan (1167-1227). Like the Huns under Attila the army of the Mongols was organised on a simple decimal system. The basic group consisted of ten mounted warriors; ten of these groups formed a Hundred; ten Hundreds were brigaded into a Thousand and ten Thousands operated as a Division. Five of these Divisions, totalling 50,000 men, nearly all mounted, came under the command of an army leader equivalent to a general. Each horseman was equipped with an iron lance and curved sabre, clothed in iron chain-mail and a leather or iron helmet. A long, light pike was sometimes carried, together with bows and arrows and small shields. The cavalry had great mobility and striking power and were used in flying horse columns to encircle an enemy. Their prey could then be eliminated with armour-piercing arrows capable of killing at distances of more than 200 yards (183 metres).

With such forces under command the Mongols conquered and ruled an empire which stretched from the Black Sea to the Pacific Ocean and it looked as if the day of the foot soldier was gone for ever.

Within the first decades of the fourteenth century there were a few isolated signals that the pendulum was swinging in the opposite direction. The mounted knights, encased in armour constituted by far the greatest part of the power of armies taking the field. The advent of artillery, served by rude artisans, was looked down upon by the cavalrymen and the infantry of the period was, on the whole, an undisciplined mob, armed with pikes, bows, halberds or clubs and clad in the ordinary garments of labourers, some of the luckier individuals owning an old rusty iron helmet and other items of cast-off military hardware. An obscure battle at Morgarten, when a small number of Swiss mountaineers, fighting on foot, vanquished a large Austrian army composed of cavalry, in 1315, served notice that armoured horsemen could be vanquished by agile and well-trained foot soldiers. Some historians generally date the demise of the mounted knight in Europe from the time of the battle of Crécy in 1346 when the English and Welsh longbowmen virtually destroyed the French cavalry charging towards their lines. The fact that gunpowder was also used, albeit with primitive ordnance and projectiles, at this battle, is not without significance.

Because of the increasing number of wars the burghers and peasants of Europe found military service distasteful and many of them preferred to pay other men to serve in their stead and, as a result, the recruitment of mercenary forces grew in popularity. This trade became a major business in Switzerland and other 'free companies' sprang up in competition; the German *Landsknechts* and Italian *Condottieri*, for example. The free companies brought to warfare the value of drill, the importance of *esprit de corps* and the first beginnings of army organisation.

An illustration of the influence of the Swiss on military thinking is the fact that soldiers of Louis XI of France first marched in step at the Camp du Pont de l'Arche in 1479-80, having been taught by Swiss drill instructors on the orders of the king. At the coronation of the same sovereign a large drum with a diameter of 30 inches (0.76m) was used to help the troops keep in step.

For three centuries variations in the use of the old Greek-style phalanx won victories for foot soldiers in Europe against cavalry charges. By constant drill Swiss on foot, moving in mass, were able to advance and manoeuvre in a tight formation. Ahead of them were levelled their long pikes which menaced enemy horsemen. It seems clear, still, that the success of a phalanx would be based on each pikeman being able to keep in step with his fellows and maintain his position in a tight formation despite rough uneven ground and gaps caused by casualties. In time, the armies of other nations copied the Swiss formations or hired mercenaries from Switzerland to fight their battles for them.

The emerging use of firearms caused the use of the Swiss phalanx to be refined by the introduction of a manoeuvre which came to be called the 'Spanish square.' This consisted of fifty men marching on a front and in file. Its success relied on a combination of pikemen with swordsmen and musketeers, each group placed for greatest tactical advantage in the square. Behind the front-rank pikemen were several lines of swordsmen, ready to dispatch the

An attack on the Saracen stronghold of Damietta (Egypt) by Crusaders, 1249. Note the foot soldiers with fifes and drums

enemy pikemen brought to bay by the Spanish front-rank men. At the corners of the square were a number of musketeers. After a single laborious loading, presenting and firing they doubled to the rear to re-load. In support of the square were cavalrymen armed with pistols. Once again, the necessity for individuals to march in step with any in close contact with their comrades would appear to have been of paramount importance in the confusion of the battlefield.

At a time when the significance in battle of drill and manoeuvre for the foot soldier was coming to be generally recognised a new word for men who marched and fought on foot came into use. The term infantry is believed to have been originally applied to a body of men collected by one of the *infantes* (princes) of Spain in the fifteenth century for the purpose of rescuing his father from the Moors. The attempt having been successful, the term was afterwards applied to foot soldiers in general, as opposed to cavalry. In 1579 a report was written about 'the *infantery* of Italy, infamous through all Europe.' This description of 'a body of foot soldiers; that part of an army which consists of men who march and manoeuvre on foot' was derived from the French *infanterie*, which in turn came from the Italian *infanteria*, *infante*, or 'youth or foot-soldier.'

The sixteenth century English infantryman was made aware of the responsibilities of his job by the introduction of a number of regulations he was expected to obey. A disciplinary code was drawn up to control the troops of the Earl of Leicester in the Netherlands in 1585. Imprisonment with loss of pay awaited a soldier found guilty of loitering with the wagons, in the hope of cadging a lift while he was supposed to be on the march. A similar punishment would be awarded to any soldier

> putting up a Hare or other Beast by making any shout or cry when marching by a field, whereby to disquiet or stay the rest of the bands, but to use all quietness and silence in their march.

Later codes were similar, including offences of marching with the baggage, straggling or pilfering on the march or breaking ranks without permission. The punishments included the bastinado as well as imprisonment. It was also laid down that troops had to cover at least ten miles a day on the march, regardless of the state and difficulties of the terrain and had to be content with supper and breakfast in the place where they spent the night.

It gradually came to be appreciated that an army could not function efficiently without drill yet no national and general system of drill was introduced in the time of Elizabeth I (nor was it until the early part of the nineteenth century). It was left to the officers in the field and at the periodical shire musters to teach the men to understand their own (officers') interpretation of the traditional commands and the corresponding evolutions. Some notes on the subject, written in 1598, said that it mattered little what commands were used as long as they were used consistently and throughout the whole army, otherwise it would breed confusion. In practice, however, there must have been substantial differences between one captain's version and the next. Several drill books were compiled during Elizabeth's reign but they were the work of private individuals and did not carry the authority of the Privy Council. They simply set down the author's idea of the existing system, with a few ideas derived from his own experiences or prejudices.

The first most comprehensive book of instruction in England was Sir John Smythe's *Instructions and Orders Mylitarie*, published in 1595. The drill commands and corresponding detail were painstakingly delineated. They covered elementary marching formations, the handling of different weapons on the march and in action and even the location of the ensign-bearers, drummers and fifers in various situations. The actual spoken orders were called 'brief speeches' but the explanation of the movements to be carried out was couched in a somewhat exaggerated style (or so it might appear to the drill instructor of today's recruits). The command 'Shoulder your pike and march!' is followed by an explanatory passage of 224 words, ending with the phrase 'and so they must all with great silence and with a grave and soldierlike grace, march.'

Generally, orders to the troops at this time could be delivered in many ways - by word of mouth, hand signals or by the sound of fife or drum. Few took the county musters of the English militia seriously and the training left much to be desired. Some officers considered that a private soldier could be well trained and made fit for war in a month. If he could not master his weapons and learn to march correctly in that time it was considered that he never would. The military writers were staunch advocates of the values of physical fitness and advised that soldiers should have plenty of running, leaping, throwing and wrestling included in their training programmes. They also advised that men should be well practised in the handling of their weapons both singly and in companies. It was also acknowledged that in some parts of the country the men were not encouraged to keep fit nor were they given proper instruction in the handling of their weapons. Some were simply marched up and down[1] and at some training sessions 'there was a useless expenditure of gunpowder.'

In Elizabeth I's reign the Privy Council ordered that a two-day instruction period should be organised for the militia in Whit week and another between then and Michaelmas. There were three sessions of training; the carrying and use of arms; marching; and the study of commands and drum signals. The men were taught when and how to give the push of pike and, in the case of firearms, the man was shown how to give his volley at the same time as his comrades. The old practice had been for the musketeers to fire together but by the end of the reign this was condemned. There was always the danger that the rear ranks would shoot those in front or that to avoid this happening they would raise their sights so high that they missed the enemy as well. The new procedure required a lot of drill to perfect and this consisted of the whole of the front rank firing simultaneously then for the second rank to pass through the first and deliver their volley in turn and so on until all the ranks had passed through and fired, by which time the original rear rank would have had the time to reload and be ready to fire again.

The introduction of firearms greatly increased the problems and cost of training. The manipulation of the pike could be readily explained to the rawest recruit and even if he failed to master the technique straightaway he could imitate those more expert in its use and master the rudiments (and remember most of them from one muster to the next). Guns were a different matter. Heavy and cumbersome and complicated to load, fire and reload correctly, they required to be used regularly and this time proved costly and difficult to arrange in peacetime.

From the sixteenth century it was held by several influential military writers that the pike was regarded as a more honourable weapon than the musket. It was, to start with, more ancient and

---

[1] A practice which, sadly, survived until fairly recently and commences with the rder of a subaltern "Give 'em a spot of drill, sergeant major!" in place of a proper aining programme.

Woodcut believed to represent some of the Devon Militia marching to repel an invasion by the French at Teignmouth (Devon) 1690

gentlemen with a taste for adventure enlisted with the sole ambition 'to trail a pike'. The pikeman was regarded in some circles as a gentleman compared with the musketeer. Pikemen were undoubtedly required to be physically stronger than the man with the musket - the weapon was long, very heavy and difficult to manoeuvre whilst the pikeman was trying to hold his pike level, at the same time endeavouring to keep in step over difficult countryside and keeping his dressing in the ranks. Pikemen had to be strong also to wear iron helmets with a ridge like a cock's comb on top, corselet or back and breast plates, as well as a gorget to protect the throat and tassets to cover the thighs. Whoever claimed superiority, on the battlefield the pikemen and musketeers needed each other's skills to survive. The best method for receiving cavalry was for the pikemen, drawn up in close order in the centre of the

formation, to be flanked by musketeers, drawn up two deep. The
first rank of the latter knelt and the second presented their muskets
over their comrades' heads. They gave fire, either both ranks
together or in succession as ordered, aiming at the oncoming
horses' legs. If the cavalry continued to charge they were brought
up short by the menacing points of the levelled pikes. The
pikemen, like the musketeers, were instructed to direct their
weapons at the horses rather than the riders. If the square was
broken the musketeers often had to use the butt end of their heavy
muskets.

Of equal importance to skill of arms the soldiers of that
period were instructed and practised in the art of marching. The
first objective was to train every man 'to observe his rank and file'
- to keep directly behind the man in front and directly abreast of
his comrades on either side. Captains were advised not to take
their men 'through fancy evolutions' that were not proper
marches. The men were to become accustomed to marching in time
with the beat of the drum and to familiarise themselves with the
basic commands transmitted by drumbeat. One of the marching
formations was forming the men into a ring as they moved
forward so that they could hear their captain's instructions more
clearly but it was considered a particularly dangerous manoeuvre
in battle as it left the ensign-bearer unprotected on the perimeter
of the ring. Other formations taught were the S or snail and the D.

As the century wore on, more drill manuals were published
and treatises printed, dealing with more complex manoeuvres and
formations but running through all the texts was the importance
attached to disciplined marching and, as the deployment of large
bodies of troops became more sophisticated, it was becoming
increasingly obvious that such matters as the length and speed of
stride and the correct dressing of rank and file could make the
difference between victory and defeat.

Chapter Three

The Development of Battlefield manoeuvres from the 16th/17th Centuries.

Throughout history the commanders responsible for training armies drew on the methods used by successful contemporaries or their predecessors. During the English Civil War (1642-1648), for example, Oliver Cromwell turned the Parliamentary Army of yeoman farmers, middle-class townsmen and artisans, 'poor tapsters and town apprentices', for the most part raw and untrained, into the splendid troops later to be known as 'The Ironsides'. He drew his ideas of training soldiers from the successful military system devised in Sweden by its king, Gustavus Adolphus (reigned 1611-1632), for a national standing army.

Cromwell instituted the idea of a basic training period of several months during which the men were drilled hard and subjected to an iron discipline. He later organised his New Model Army on the plan of his Ironsides and dressed them in scarlet coats with facings bearing regimental colours, a uniform which became traditional wear for the British infantryman for the next two and a half centuries. Despite his unpopularity in Royalist and other circles Cromwell was an excellent military leader and be truly said to be the father of the British Army.

With the introduction of newer weapons the handling of arms came to take as much time, if not more, than marching and foot drill. When Queen Anne came to the throne in 1702 infantry-men were still armed with the long, heavy pike and the clumsy matchlock musket but two years later the pike had been abolished as a basic weapon and the foot soldier carried the improved flintlock, with bayonet. The musket fired a lead ball, about an ounce in weight, by means of six drams of powder, the whole being made up into a cartridge in stout paper. Loading procedure, which was reduced to a drill, was to open the pan, tear the cartridge open with the teeth, prime the pan and close it. The charge, ball, and remaining paper (which helped to hold the loose ball in place in the barrel) was rammed down the bore by means of a ramrod.

The soldier was expected to prime, load and fire his weapon correctly and had to obey twenty-one different words of command whilst doing so. When fully trained he could achieve a rate of fire of two rounds a minute. In the face of enemy cannon fire and musketry and affected by thick smoke and the noise of battle, drumbeats and confused shouting around him, it was only the well-drilled foot soldier who would be able to march forward resolutely in correct formation and step and carry out meticulously the orders he could barely hear to enable him to discharge his musket effectively.

Everything depended on the marching ability, exact drill and weapon handling of each soldier. The armies of the eighteenth century consisted of masses of troops belonging to a variety of regiments, sometimes from different countries, each of which would probably differ in training and manoeuvre from the others. When an army neared the enemy it first had to shake itself out from the order of march to a line of battle.

There was usually a dignified an unhurried deployment into line, sometimes accompanied by bands playing, colours flying and every man in step, keeping his position exactly and looking straight to his front. The movements of the infantry were covered by their cavalry, artillery, and skirmishers operating in front of the battle line and the procedure might take hours to complete to the commander's satisfaction.

When the respective commanders had completed their dispositions, having studied the nature of the terrain, the obstacles which might impede the movement of their armies, in the form of marshy ground, sunken roads, 'dead' ground and thick woods, battle was joined.

Even at this stage, before the first shots had been fired, a commander, lacking determination, could very well give the orders to his troops to disengage and turn from the field, leaving his exasperated opposite number the task of ordering his forces to resume a column of route and give chase. If both commanders were determined to fight and had completed their dispositions, the armies would be drawn up in solid lines, facing each other across a gap of only a few hundred yards, depending on the effective range of each other's artillery. The dressing of the lines of infantry was accomplished and maintained by the rolling of drums or shouted orders, aided, sometimes, by the sergeants lining up the men by pushing them into position with the shafts of their halberds or spontoons and, on occasion, by the flat of their officers' sword blades.

The colours and bands finally took their correct places in the formation and the officers, according to their ranks, aligned themselves in front of, in or behind the firing line and waited for their commander's order to commence hostilities. (One observer of such a set-piece preliminary to battle noted that in the last few minutes, before firing started, the men of both armies took the opportunity of relieving themselves in their positions.) In some armies there was a practice of chaplains giving a general absolution to all ranks before battle was joined.

The light troops or 'skirmishers' of both sides were the first to fire before the general engagement and, after a scattered exchange of musketry with their counterparts or the front rank of opposing infantry, they retired rapidly between the ranks of their own troops.

It was then the turn of the artillery and the ground seemed to be covered with bouncing and rolling shot, apart from the projectiles which tore through the lines of troops. Both types of fire left great gaps full of dead and wounded and the survivors had to side-step left and right or march forward to close ranks.

After the first shock of the artillery bombardment it was the turn of the infantry to attack. They marched forward, with drums beating, their muskets shouldered and only when they came within effective range were they ordered to present their pieces and open fire.

At first it was the general practice for armies to fire their muskets in rotation by rank, the first one or two ranks lowering their weapons and firing, aiming at the middle of the enemy soldiers facing them. They would then retire to reload whilst the rear ranks would take their places and fire. Later, the famous British commander Marlborough introduced a system of platoons grouped in 'firings' in which there was a greater concentration of volleys, better directed and controlled by the regimental officers.

Despite the efficacy of Marlborough's infantry fire tactics the long and laborious business of deploying great masses of men and horses from long marching into a line of battle was not a pretty sight and most unlike the neat diagrams in the contemporary drill manuals. Because of the lack of a uniform drill book it was not possible at that time to perform manoeuvres of forming and wheeling on the march so they had to be done at the halt, by means of screamed orders, frantic beating of drums and sometimes thwacking on backs from spontoons or sword blades. To Wellington's officers a century later and certainly to modern eyes, the deployment of Marlborough's forces, although relatively most effective at the time, would appear something like a shambles. After being shaken into line there was nothing wrong with the musketry at the battle of Ramillies in 1706. It was reported that the smoke from the rolling volleys of fire of Marlborough's infantry extended a distance of four miles - a phenomenon which was not to be seen again until the time of Frederick the Great of Prussia.

The success of Marlborough could not have been achieved without intensive practice in drill, manoeuvre and musketry being undertaken by his officers, sergeants and privates. Battalions were usually drawn up with their officers ranged in front and the colonel on foot, about eight or ten paces to the front, with sword drawn, opposite the centre of his battalion, with his best drummer standing alongside him. (The colonel was advised to take special care to keep in front of the two centre platoons while the other platoons were discharging their volleys and, of course, when it came to the turn of the centre platoons, it was in his best interests to step aside and only return to the centre when the men had ceased firing and were reloading.) When the colonels found that there was no avoiding a battle they ordered their soldiers to lay down their knapsacks, tent poles and other heavy items not required for the battle and the sergeants would arrange for them to be collected and deposited in a safe place.

It was realised that not every colonel had a voice capable of being heard in the noise of battle so the sound of the drum was all-important. The main signals were a preparatory 'Take Care!' indicated by the drummer beating a ruffle (a vibrating beat); 'March!' in which time was beaten, and 'Halt!' which involved speedy preparations to open fire:

> Drummer beats a preparative, upon which the six platoons of the first firing make ready....Front rank kneels, placing butts of muskets on the ground by their left feet, ready for next word of command or signal of drum....Drummer beats a flam [a loud emphatic double beat] whereupon the front rank drops muzzles to the ground and two rear ranks present....Further flam, platoons fire and recover their arms, fall back and load as fast as they can.

The successful tactics of marching, manoeuvre and musketry carried out by Marlborough's troops were noted by Leopold I, Prince of Anhalt-Dessau (1676-1747). He was a Prussian field marshal and was responsible for the reorganisation of the Prussian Army in the years preceding the notable successes of Frederick the Great (reigned from 1740-1786). He was aware of the importance of cavalry and artillery but considered them secondary to the infantry. The thorough training devised by the 'Old Dessauer' led to their high reputation throughout the world for nearly two centuries. Training was founded on the most rigid, sometimes harsh discipline. A system of fire control was introduced, similar, but more polished, to that used in Marlborough's army. Prussian infantry were taught to execute rapid, cadenced and mechanical movements while on the march, charging their muskets and firing. The movements were practised again and again until the troops were able to carry them out with liveliness and unified rhythm. This was emphasised by the sound of their boot heels striking the

*An artist's impression of Prussian infantry advancing in line,
18th century*

round as one and the noise of their hands striking their muskets at
the same time. This came to be the universal method of handling
weapons and foot drill but until it was perfected by the troops
trained by the 'Old Dessauer' no-one had exploited this so

successfully nor obtained such accurate and devastating salvoes whilst advancing.

The reputation of the Prussian Army did not depend only on its marching ability and fighting qualities but also on its smartness. Frederick William I of Prussia, the father of Frederick the Great, also laid foundations of the invincible Prussian Army of the time. He combed Europe for gigantic men for his Grenadier Regiment and fitted them each year in brand-new uniforms. They wore blue jackets embroidered with ornamental fastenings of gold with red facings and cuffs, while the waistcoat and breeches were of straw-coloured cloth, and the spatterdashes or gaiters white. The headdress was the tall sugar-loaf cap.

Under Frederick the Great the infantry nearly always marched in columns of platoons, taking full advantage of the width of the ill-defined roads of the time. Cavalry columns moved on the wings of the advance and the artillery and baggage were kept in the centre of the column. Footsore soldiers were piled on to baggage wagons and non-commissioned officers were ordered to accompany all soldiers who had to step out of the ranks to relieve themselves. A small rearguard followed the marching columns, sweeping up deserters and stragglers.

Frederick's army was capable of marching a dozen miles a day for a week or two at a stretch. In normal circumstances half of that distance was a more reasonable average, given the exigencies of supply and the necessity of resting for one day in three or four. The rate sank still further in the spring and autumn because of the shortness of the days and the heavy rainfall which flooded the earth roads and open country.

Foreign observers were impressed by the excellence of Prussian marching and manoeuvre but things did go wrong on occasion. One witness described how a battalion of 200 or 250 files made a fine picture as it advanced on a broad front. He wrote of the soldiers' legs with their light coloured gaiters working back and forth like a warp on a weaver's frame, while the sun's rays were reflected from the polished muskets and the whitened leather equipment of the men. It needed only a ploughed field or a churned-up meadow to destroy this picture.

PLATOON VOLLEY FIRING OF THE ARMIES OF MARLBOROUGH AND FREDERICK THE GREAT

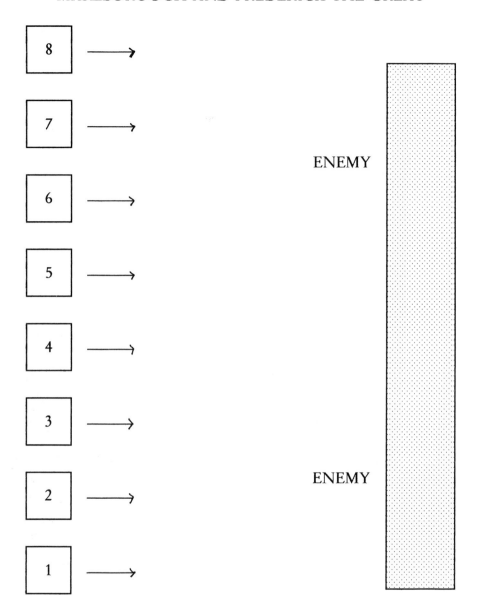

PLATOON FIRE TACTICS ensured that there was a continual loosing off of volleys and a reserve of loaded muskets always ready to fire. Firing was delivered by platoons of battalion in the order 1,8,2,7,3,6,4 and 5 (numbering from the right). The flanking platoons were then ready to fire again.

Some of the soldiers would lose step or their dressing and their comrades would unwittingly follow suit. Within a few yards the straight line would begin to buckle and fragment and it would need superhuman efforts by the officers, NCOs and drummers to get the advance going again in unison and correct alignment. (A record was probably established in 1785 when Frederick assembled practically the whole of his army for a great military review. 29 battalions marched forward in one line and it was estimated that the distance from one wing to the other was about four miles [6.44 km]. It is not recorded how far this amazing formation marched forward but it is unlikely that cohesion could be maintained for more than a few hundred yards at a time.)

The Prussian Army was trained in the complicated tactics of platoon fire, a refinement of the methods of Marlborough and Anhalt-Dessau. This ensured that there was a continual loosing off of volleys and a reserve of loaded muskets always ready to fire. Platoon fire was delivered by the platoons of the battalion in the order 1,8,2,7,3,6,4 and 5. Numbering from the right this meant that volleys were delivered from either flank of the battalion towards the centre then the flanking platoons would be ready to fire again and so on. A battalion could fire at the halt and on the march.

Experience soon showed that the niceties of platoon fire were impracticable in battle conditions and after two or three orderly volleys had been fired confusion would set in, what with the noise of battle, the smoke, the beating of drums, shouted orders, nearby casualties from enemy cannon or musket fire, faults in reloading, hang-fires, ranks and files becoming mixed up, front ranks failing to kneel and being pushed aside or trying to get to the rear and so on. A situation could, and many times did develop to the point where everybody seemed to be blazing away at once and the officers and NCOs, no matter how they shouted or struck their men, found it impossible to control the fire. Once this had happened the whole line, seemingly of its own volition would either set itself in motion to move forward or back or, disastrously, to break into groups which could easily be at the mercy of a determined line of enemy infantry.

As if the difficulties of maintaining a line were not enough, even on the parade ground, the Prussian soldier found that he was expected to master more intricate manoeuvres. One particular refinement adopted by Frederick the Great was a method of deploying a column of troops into line. The soldiers would keep their shoulders rigidly to the front while the feet executed a dance-like step. If, for instance, the movement was to be to the right, then the right foot went forward first, the left foot was crossed over the right, the right foot went forward again and so on, resulting in an oblique direction of march until the final position was reached. The Prussian battle tactics became the basis for the organisation of European armies and, later, the American Army after the Revolution, for the next century and a half. As well as imitating the drill and tactics, similar uniforms and equipment, even the use of a particular hair powder, were adopted throughout the western world.

In the Austrian Army of Maria Theresa, during the Seven Years' War (1756-1763), for example, special drills were devised for almost every eventuality, in common with those taught in the Prussian Army. 'Hedge firing', when the enemy was lurking behind hedges or brushwood, or firing outward when they themselves were caught when marching along a sunken road or along a track through a thick wood, were all practised in regular field exercises. Although observers reported that the Austrian Army looked splendid under arms, being smartly dressed, fully equipped and well-armed and was composed of tall, fit soldiers, it was said by some that it did not know how to move correctly. A line of Austrian infantry could not, apparently, advance three hundred paces without losing its alignment and intervals and fell into hopeless confusion - a thing, the critics observed, which could not conceivably have happened in the Prussian Army. It was also said that the Austrians could not march without getting strung out and made a hopeless mess, sometimes, when forming into line from column. On one occasion it was noticed that the advance in battle order during one engagement was executed far too slowly, to the accompaniment of much chatter and the ranks were out of alignment all along the front.

On the march men of the Austrian Army were allowed to take off the stiff and uncomfortable stocks around their necks and tie them round their arms and were also allowed to hang their swords over their shoulders so as not to bang their calves, and even undo some of their waistcoat buttons. Against this apparent slackness, however, on forced marches, the soldiers had to put up with being directed through water and boggy patches, even when they could have marched, dry-shod, around the sides. The progress of the army did not permit such time-wasting diversions. The only things that mattered on these occasions were the speed of the march and the correct alignment of the columns.

The ordinary unforced march was a comparatively leisurely affair, which allowed the bakers time to prepare their bread. There was a complete rest on every third or fourth day and an average daily progress of something like six or eight miles. Troops were driven much faster if they belonged to a corps entrusted with a particular important enterprise. One Austrian commander's troops covered an average of fifteen miles a day on a raid on Berlin in 1757 and another corps attained more than twenty miles a day to reach the same capital in 1760 after a march of 200 miles.

Whatever the speed or length of march the soldiers were kept under close watch when they passed through woods or villages lest anyone should take it into his head to slip away. For the same reason the filling of the men's water-flasks was usually entrusted to corporals and a few reliable men.

The principle of keeping a close watch on the rank and file in the process of deploying troops prior to a battle is succinctly expressed in a British drill manual of the early eighteenth century. After setting out the positions to be occupied when a battalion was drawn up on the battlefield, three deep, their bayonets fixed on their muskets and so on, the instruction goes on to say that 'the battalion being thus formed for battle and as it were riveted together so that no soldier can possibly misbehave but there will be an eye presently upon him.'

In 1809, during the retreat of the British Army to Corunna, Brigadier General Robert Craufurd of the Light Brigade saw two men straggling away from the main body. It was in the early stages of the march and he knew that he had to do his utmost to keep his troops together. He halted the column, ordered a drumhead court martial on the spot and the two men were sentenced to two hundred lashes each. Some of the troops were becoming careless and ruffianly in their demeanour, others were in tears from their bleeding feet and others were weak with dysentery from the effects of eating bad food they had acquired on the march. The punishment awarded the stragglers, brutal as it might seem, seemed to stiffen the resolve of most of the infantry and they struggled to keep formation during the rest of the retreat.

Three years later, after Craufurd had been killed in the breach at Ciudad Rodrigo, he was buried on the spot where he had fallen. As his men of the Light Division marched back to camp they waded through a large pond which lay in their path instead of wasting time walking around it. This was their tribute to the memory of their commander who would yell 'Sit down in it, Sir, sit down in it!' to any of his men trying to avoid getting wet by stepping round a puddle and so wasting time and breaking the ranks.

During the Napoleonic Wars and especially in the Iberian Peninsula the French attacked in heavy columns, each with a shoulder-to-shoulder frontage of perhaps fifty to sixty men and a depth of as many as eighty men. Viewed from the front the columns, with their colours flying, drums beating and men cheering, looked menacing but to a trained enemy the formation, viewed from any angle, presented a target of upwards of forty yards long and over five feet high. The British and Prussian line formations opposing the French columns had every advantage, nearly all their muskets being able to fire into the front and flanks of the mass of advancing infantry, only the front ranks of the latter being able to fire effectively. Heavy casualties were often inflicted and as the volley fire could take place every fifteen to twenty seconds, the carnage inflicted was considerable. As the surviving Frenchmen tried to retreat their comrades behind sometimes attempted to push forward to use their weapons and a hopeless confusion resulted.

The familiar battle tactics were at first tried during the American Civil War (1861-1865) with both sides unleashing massive infantry attacks, with bayonets fixed, in the Napoleonic manner but the resultant disasters, because of the increased range and accuracy of firearms, caused a change in tactics. Soldiers learned to spread out, to advance in rushes and to take advantage of any cover that was available: a tree trunk, a sunken road or ditch. In the war from then on, despite the major change in tactics, the ability of infantry to march rapidly and in good order was still of paramount importance. It was thanks to the Confederate General Nathan Bedford Forrest (1821-77) and his picturesque phrase 'getting there fustest with the mostest' that later commanders learned how to achieve success in war.

An observer of German infantry in the Franco-Prussian War of 1870-71 stated that they marched in a somewhat open and irregular column of fours, the interval between files being specially intended 'to give room for a peculiar swinging gait which carried the men across the ground with ease and rapidity.' The German soldiers were described as strong, lusty fellows, comparatively lightly equipped and it was reported that they strode by with an elastic step.

For some years, also, the British infantryman had won a fine reputation for his dogged marching ability. This was particularly the case in the heat and dust of India in the days before the railways had been fully developed. Under carefully organised programmes regiments were often weeks, sometimes months, on the march from one part of the country to another, moving across arid plains and up the winding passes of the North-West Frontier. These marches hardened the men and made them familiar with the pitching and breaking of camps and the loading and management of mules and other beasts of burden.

The Field Exercise and Evolutions of Infantry instructions issued by H.M. Stationery Office in 1877 emphasised that the success of military operations depended in a great measure upon the compact and well-regulated order of march in the several columns of the army. On all occasions, when marching out of camp or quarters or when moving after a regular halt upon the march, each corps would march off by word of command, and with music, unless the contrary was ordered. The men were to be silent, keep their dressing and maintain the step, as if marching on parade, until the command 'March at Ease!' was given by the commanding officer of the regiment and repeated by the captains. When marching at ease the ranks could be opened and the files loosened; but each rank, section or company would be kept perfectly distinct and every man was to remain in his place. On the command 'Attention!' the men would slope (or trail) their arms and take up the step, perfect order and silence being resumed until the word was again given to march at ease.

No man was to quit the ranks for any purpose whatsoever, without permission from his captain. Men who obtained permission to fall out for any other cause other than illness, would invariably leave their packs and arms, to be carried by the section to which they belonged, until they returned to the ranks.

The 1877 infantry instructions manual was of little use in the British disaster of 1879 when a Zulu force annihilated a battalion of the 24th Foot (The South Wales Borderers). Because of the ineptitude of their commanders the British fought in open formation instead of their usual squares and suffered the ultimate penalty.

In the early decades of the nineteenth century the South African territories today known as Zululand and Natal were studded with great military kraals garrisoned by powerful warlike regiments. Under the tyrannical rule of Shaka, King of the Zulus, the warriors were welded into an all-conquering force which overwhelmed other African armies. The young Zulus as children learned to throw wooden spears until they could hit any small animal at a distance and they also enjoyed stick-fighting. By the time they were 17 or 18 years old they could run fifty miles in a day, jogging and sprinting. When the time came for them to live in military kraals their training was intensified and they were advised to throw away their sandals and run in bare feet across rough and thorny ground, to harden the soles of their feet. Shaka dispensed with the light throwing spear and invented a heavier weapon with a wide blade for close-quarter fighting. The men were taught to batter an opponent with their ox-hide shields then stab him in the left breast.

The Zulu army (*impi*) numbered about 20,000 men, divided into regiments according to age-groups and, because the men of each group had known each other since boyhood there was a spirit of great rivalry and keen competition between them. Each regiment was attired differently, except for a basic uniform of skin head-bands, war-kilts of rolled civet and monkey-skins and their arms and legs decorated with oxtail tufts. Regiments could be identified at a glance by the colour of their oxtail shields and the plumes in their headdress.

The army marched into regimental columns, with scouts in advance, on the flanks and in the rear. The young soldiers carried their own mats and belongings, with shields rolled up and carried on the backs. The veteran warriors and commanders had carriers for their belongings and a herd of cattle was driven along on the flanks of the main body. At the beginning of the march girls carried beer, corn and other food for their male relatives and when this was exhausted the girls returned home.

The Zulus could march with remarkable swiftness and if they came to a river in full flood which was out of their depth but was not too wide, they plunged into in a dense mass, holding on to one another, those behind pushing the others forward and very few men were lost.

On reaching hostile territory or when in broken country the army marched in closer formation. Scouts were sent forward to locate the enemy and when they returned with information the warriors were sprinkled with a potion which, they were told, would make them invulnerable to bullets.

After a briefing by their commanders the army was allotted its disposition for attack - this took the form of a crescent or semi-circle with two horns, a main body (a centre) and a reserve (the 'loins'). The tactics usually included a feint with one horn while the other, concealed in the bush or long grass, swept round to surround the enemy. The centre, composed of the greatest number of men and the most experienced, then advanced to crush the enemy. Behind them was the reserve which came into action when

Artist's impression of the enveloping 'horn' of a Zulu impi closing on the enemy

the centre was in difficulty or joined in the pursuit of the fleeing enemy. The 'loins' sat with their backs to the developing battle so that they would not become excited and charge precipitately before they were ordered to move. When the enveloping tactic was used the Zulus first jogged then sprinted towards the enemy, stabbing with their heavy spears, usually called assegais and sometimes, but not always, hurling the lighter spears they also carried. They also smashed heads with heavy wooden clubs (knobkerries).

By the time of the battle of Isandhlwana many of the Zulu warriors possessed firearms but, fortunately for the British and their other enemies, they did not change their tactics to make effective use of them. Shortly after the British defeat another force confronted the Zulus near their capital Ulundi. On this occasion the British used their favourite formation of the square, with cavalry inside and, at the appropriate moment, a side of the square opened to allow the horsemen to charge and overcome their ferocious opponents, bringing an end to the war.

The 1914 Field Service Pocket Book, issued just before the outbreak of the 1914-1918 Great War, prescribed that an average march under normal conditions for a large column of troops was to be fifteen miles a day. Small columns were expected to cover 25 miles a day under favourable conditions. It was laid down that four men should march abreast and columns of fours would march on the left side of the road unless direct orders to the contrary were issued.

More detailed instructions were contained in the Infantry Training Manual of 1926. It was emphasised that the foundation of good marching discipline was keeping step and this, together with exact covering, dressing and the maintenance of the prescribed distance from the man in front, would be insisted upon even when marching at ease. Platoon commanders would arrange for short lectures to be given to their men on the importance of march discipline, the orders to be observed during the march, how smoking affected endurance and how thirst was aggravated rather than reduced by frequent recourse to the water-bottle. A battalion which was slack in march was generally slack in battle. Want of march discipline had been the cause of battalions being unable, through fatigue, to take part in a battle after a march. Halts would be made for ten minutes at ten minutes to every clock hour, irrespective of the hour of the start or the nearness of the end of the march.

Every man in four would change places after each ten minutes' halt. The men originally on the inner flank would fall in on the other flank and the remainder of the four moving to their left or right. Every man would take his equipment off during each clock-hour halt and put it on again at one minute before re-starting. Under suitable conditions troops should be made to lie down during halts and, if possible, raise their feet to relieve them of pressure and allow the flow of blood to circulate. Organised singing on the march would be encouraged as it helped men to march well even when fatigued. The more tired the troops became towards the end of the march, the more strictly would march discipline be enforced.

The 1935 Manual of Elementary Drill was broadly the same as the 1926 manual but added that slackness in march discipline not only caused discomfort in the unit itself but might cause disaster because of troops arriving late or too exhausted to take an effective part in battle, or through roads becoming congested and blocked. March discipline which broke down at a time of crisis was of little value; the longer and more trying the march, the more strictly would it be enforced. A reference to the possibility of a wider use of chemical weapons being exploited by an enemy in the future was the order that when men removed their equipment at the clock-hour halt the anti-gas respirator in its haversack would not be taken off.

Despite the introduction of columns of motorised infantry in most European armies before the outbreak of the Second World War in 1939, the infantry of most countries were still expected to march long distances in all kinds of terrain. Although there was much publicity accorded to the German Army for its armoured 'blitzkreig' tactics in Poland and France in 1939-40 it was a fact that German infantry, with their horse-drawn transport (as did their Soviet counterparts from June 1941) were called upon to march considerable distances to consolidate the gains of their armoured vanguards. In the Polish campaign some regiments marched as much as thirty miles a day, for days on end, to engage the Polish armies and hold them close to their frontiers. These distances were often exceeded in the later drive through France.

Although modern armies do not generally include long route marches along roads and across rough or mountainous country in their training programmes, circumstances sometimes arise when infantry could be called upon to undertake marching across unsuitable terrain for considerable distances and some otherwise outstandingly fit formations have been found wanting in their ability and determination to close with the enemy after a strenuous approach march. Thousands of pounds in compensation were paid out to members of the Royal Marine Commandos who had contracted a form of 'trench foot', apparently caused by exposure to cold and wet during the Falklands Campaign of 1982. Much criticism was directed towards the formerly trusty British ammunition army boot but it is possible that the condition might have been due to a lack of emphasis on the care of the feet in training and a disregard of the principles of foot hygiene by the men themselves and their supervising officers.

With the present-day approach of hard and fast endurance marches and runs there is always the chance that when the feet of the modern soldier (or Marine) are exposed to the challenge of travelling across rocky or soggy ground for miles at a time, they will let him down. Old soldiers know that when the feet have become used to the punishment of travelling mile after mile on uneven ground or hard roads, week after week, in all kinds of weather, they will become hardened and able to endure all sorts of difficulties in the future.

The Second Dragoons (Royal Scots Greys)
at Blenheim 1704. Dragoons rode on horseback
to the battlefield then dismounted and fought as infantry.

Chapter Four

The Individual Training of Infantrymen in Marching Skills and Tactics.

With the development of the intricate battlefield manoeuvres of the eighteenth century and later it became plain that all depended on the individual skills of the troops in foot drill, marching and the concerted use of their weapons.

The purpose of all drill was to turn the soldiers into automata in the shortest time available, capable of performing a number of functions in close-order tactics. The recruit was taught first to stand correctly and turn at the halt, then to march, using the correct length of stride, keeping in step with his comrades and moving as one with them in the various evolutions. He was then instructed how to hold his weapon, whether it was a musket or pike, first at the halt and then on the march.

A great deal of thought was devoted to the problem of the length of stride in marching. The distance covered in each step was such as would not demand great exertion and could be equally adapted to men of large and small stature. The step of a disciplined soldier had to be of uniform length, to ensure equality of gait in line or column. Eventually the length of step was computed as being thirty inches (76.2cm). Throughout the seventeenth century the normal marching pace of the English foot soldier was the slow and steady 'Pikeman's step', which differed from the sometimes brisker march tempo of Continental troops. The soldier was expected to obey the voice of the drum and, to regularise the pace throughout the army, a certain measure was beaten at Greenwich in 1610, in the presence of Prince Henry, the brother of the future Charles I.

Marlborough quickened the normal English pace but even then it was a slower tempo than the present 'quick' but not as slow as the modern 'slow' march.

The European armies kept a close watch on the foot drill and manoeuvres of their allies and potential enemies by sending observers to watch the drill and exercises being carried out by their counterparts. If any good or new ideas were noted they would be either modified or included in the training methods of the troops back home. The length of step, for example, did not vary by more than an inch or so from country to country.

Before the introduction of the standardised drill manual in the British Army the system of teaching a recruit the right way to march more often than not took the form of a sergeant showing a squad the correct way to march then getting the soldiers to imitate him. If an awkward man did not pick up the rudiments of a movement quickly enough the instructor would probably seize hold of him roughly and show him the drill again.

In the Prussian Army, in the time of Frederick the Great, those responsible for the instruction of men had far more latitude. regimental commanders were permitted to strike soldiers with sticks or fists for making a half-turn too early, too late or not showing enough 'snap' in their drill. Offences punishable in this way included men having spots of mud on their gaiters or failing to polish their buttons. One recorded instance describes how an officer knocked out six of a grenadier's teeth because he did not hold his head up straight enough when ordered.

British Army lore includes the tale that recruits for the militia, most of whom were agricultural labourers, apparently unable to tell their left from their right, were instructed to tie a few stalks of hay around one ankle and stalks of straw round the other. They were then ordered to march in the correct way by shouts of 'Hay, straw, hay, straw!' and so on. Other methods would of course have to be devised to teach the lads from towns how to march as the difference in the appearance of hay and straw would probably have eluded them.[1]

---

[1] As late as 1943 some American Army recruits did not know their left feet or arms from their right so instructors tied coloured ribbons around the limbs of the recruits.

An officer of a Prussian infantry regiment 1738. He is carrying the half-pike (or spontoon) as a symbol of his authority, a means of ensuring straight lines in the troops under his command and, on occasion, an offensive weapon in battle

The first documentary evidence of a prescribed pace in the Prussian Army dates from 1747 when it was recommended that at the start of an advance a rate of 90-95 steps to the minute would be ordered but after that 70-75 steps would be fast enough. The measure of the pace was practised so often that it became imprinted in the soldiers' brains and their legs became accustomed to the right speed. He learned to take no notice of the drum and fife if they sounded the wrong time.[2]

The legs of the Prussian soldier were kept stiff during the march, with the toe sweeping close to the ground, rather like today's British Army slow march. As a means of progression it was easy and untiring and looked like the natural pace of a man walking deliberately and solemnly towards some objective.

The Prussian line infantry were packed in extremely tight formation. They were at first closed up so that the right arm of one man was positioned behind the left, musket-carrying arm of his comrade to his right. Later a more comfortable but still crowded position of elbow-to-elbow was introduced, only one foot ten inches being allowed for each man's space. The gap between the ranks of soldiers varied between two paces and a mere one foot (30cm approx).

Following an enactment in 1757, two regiments of Militia were raised in Hampshire, composed of men of parishes chosen by lot and compelled to serve for three years. Traditionally, the Militia had been made up of citizens who regarded themselves, and were so regarded, sometimes by cruel caricature or lampoon as citizens or countrymen first and soldiers second. An old Hampshire song gives a good-humoured slant to a situation, not always appreciated by a young rustic unlucky in the parish ballot. The song also gives a picture of the type of training sometimes given to the young and raw militiamen.

---

[2] Even without a stopwatch former soldiers who served in the infantry can regulate their walking pace to about three miles an hour, or about 116-120 steps a minute, if they are reasonably fit and had been drilled rigorously when they were young men.

The Good Militia Man
by Honest Dan, the Plough-boy turned Soldier

I was a plough-boy tall, Sir,
My name was Honest Dan;
But at my country's call, Sir, I've turned Militia man.

So on our little green, Sir,
Away from all the mire,
I daily now am seen, Sir,
To cock, present and fire.

In regimentals bright, Sir,
Of scarlet I do shine,
With hair tied up so tight, Sir,
And whitened all so fine.

Of maidens not a few, Sir,
Come crowding round the green;
And so do parents too, Sir,
The children push between.

There like a soldier prime, Sir,
I march both quick and slow;
I stamp my foot in time, Sir,
And then kick up my toe.

Meanwhile with sound so grand, Sir,
They beat the rum-drum-drum;
'Till all our valiant band, Sir,
Do wish the French would come.

The writer, Sir Walter Besant (1836-1901) in one of his historical novels, described the men of a Militia regiment stationed in Portsmouth in the early nineteenth century:

They came to us, raw country lads, with their
country lurch upon them, their good-natured country grin and their insatiable thirst for beer....These
rustics of militiamen, I declare, after a few weeks
were as well set up, pipe-clayed and drilled as any
regiment of the line. In one thing, one must needs
to confess, they were inferior to the regulars. It was
not in perpendicularity, which they easily acquired.
We were still in the pipe-clay days, when the white
belt and cross shoulder-straps were daily stiffened by
that abominable stuff; the white trousers of summer
had also to be kept in a white sepulchre of purity
by the same means; a man who is pipe-clayed cannot
stoop; the black leather collar kept the head at an
unbending line with the body; and the yellow tufts
on the shoulder, with the swallow-tails of the absurd
regimental coat and the tiny ball of red stuff on the
regimental hat all combined to necessitate a carriage
ten times stiffer and more rigidly upright than in
these degenerate days [1870s]. The most lurcher-like
of rustics was bound to become perpendicular. But
their failing was in the way they took their beer.
The old regular got drunk as often as the militiaman
but the drunker he got the stiffer he grew so that
when he was quite helpless he fell like a lamp-post,
with uncompromising legs. And we, who knew by
experience how a soldier should fall, remarked with
sorrow rather than anger that the militiaman fell in
a heap like a ploughboy, and so betrayed his cus-
tomary pursuits.

This excellently-written piece illustrates perfectly the prevailing
attitude of most of his compatriots towards the militiaman - the
constant references to 'lurcher-like' rustics, for instance, - yet
contains the acknowledgement that it was possible for much
apparently unsuitable material to be turned into well-drilled
soldiers. There is much information about the clothing and

equipment of a soldier of that period which must have contributed little to his comfort at drill, on the march or in action.

The correct position of standing at attention was always the first essential of drill taught to the recruit, whether he belonged to the Regular Army, Marines or Militia. It was considered most important as it was from this position that any march step would begin.

In a drill book of 1766 for the Marine Volunteer, written by a lieutenant of H.M. Marine Forces, he stated that when recruits came to quarters they should, before being supplied with arms and accoutrements, be taught to stand and walk in an erect and easy attitude:

> A Soldier with Arms must be silent, steady and particularly attentive to the Words of Command; without which it is impossible for him to perform his Exercise, Firings and Movements, with any degree of Exactness and Propriety. He is to stand straight, square and firm, not making the least Motion with Head, Body, Hands or Feet, but when ordered; his Toes turned outwards, the Heels in a Line and a Hand's Breadth asunder, which is about four Inches; [the author, in a footnote, disapproved of 'the modern method of standing with the Heels close because I do not think it possible for a Man to stand so firm, as in the Manner prescribed, wherefore he cannot handle his Arms with equal Dexterity.'] the Musket carried perpendicularly, on the Left Shoulder, the Barrel to the Front, the Butt in the Left palm, pressed close to the Body, a little below the Hip-Bone, the Fore-Finger above the Swell; the Left Arm not extended, but with a little Reserve, in order to make every Motion convenient and easy to the Soldier.
>
> All Words of Command should be given with a distinct audible Voice, and a short Pause made where the Words are stopped, in order to give

the Men Time to recollect what is to be done. No
Soldier to begin a Motion until the exercising
Officer utters the last Syllable of the Sentence.

A former sergeant in the Royal Welsh Fusiliers recalled that in 1773, then aged seventeen, he joined the regiment and was put into the hands of a drill sergeant to be taught how to walk and step out like a soldier. The lad hated the exercise and for three weeks he was drilled four hours each day. After his drill was adjudged satisfactory he was issued with a set of equipment and a firelock and was marched every day from his barracks to a bowling green nearby, to be instructed in musketry exercises. He thought that when he underwent exercises in drill and musketry it was the most disagreeable part of soldiering. He confessed that some of his old drill sergeants were unnecessarily, if not wantonly, severe.

A lieutenant of the 70th Regiment of Foot composed a drill book in 1777 in which the position of standing to attention under arms was more accurately defined. The soldier was not to make the slightest motion with his head, body, feet or hands but would stand straight and firm upon his legs, his head turned to the right, heels close, toes a little turned out, the belly drawn in a little but without constraint, the breast a little projected, shoulders square to the front and kept back.

In 1775 America started to fight for its independence against Great Britain. For some years the revolutionary forces were little more than a group of civilians fighting Indian-style against well-trained, highly-disciplined British redcoats. The hardships and losses suffered by the colonials stemmed from the lack of a military tradition in the country. Recognising the crisis General Washington enlisted the aid of a Prussian officer - Baron Friedrich von Steuben, a former staff officer in the army of Frederick the Great. He arrived at Valley Forge in 1778 and inspected an army of several thousand half-starved wretched men in rags. He commented that a European army could not be kept together in such a state. He set to work immediately and wrote drill movements and regulations at night and taught them the following day to a model company of 120 men selected from the line.

The men learned discipline and how to respond to a command without hesitation. They grew in confidence and soon learned to perfect the fifteen one-second movements required to load and fire muskets.

Later, the model company was distributed throughout the army to teach the drill they had learned. Through this means they improved the overall effectiveness and efficiency of the regiments.

During the American revolutionary War period the troops marched at a cadence of 76 paces to the minute.

In the *Instruction for the Drill and the Method of Performing the Eighteen Movements,* written by an ensign and adjutant of the First Battalion of the Royal Army of Reserve in 1803 the position of the soldier standing without arms was improved still further. After the observation that 'care should be taken to supple the Recruit and banish the air of the Rustic', caution was sounded about 'the Excess of Setting Up, which stiffened the Person and tended to throw the Body backwards instead of forward, would be carefully avoided, as being contrary to every Principle of Move-ment.' The exact requirements were then delineated:

> The equal squareness of the shoulders and body to
> the front was the first and great principle of a
> soldier. The heels were to be in a line and closed -
> the knees straight, without stiffness - the toes a little
> turned out, so that the feet might form an angle of
> about sixty degrees. The arms were to hang near the
> body but not stiff - the flat part of the hand and
> little finger touching the thigh; the thumbs as far
> back as the seams of the breeches; the elbows and
> shoulders were to be kept back; the belly rather
> drawn in and the breast advanced, but without
> constraint, the body upright but inclining forward,
> so that the weight of it principally bore on the front
> part of the feet. The head was to be kept erect and
> neither turned to the right nor to the left.

After the correct position of attention had been taught the recruits moved to the more difficult subject of marching correctly. Once again the practice was for the instructor to demonstrate a perfect marching step, usually by means of a 'balance step' wherein the movement of marching was broken up into individual stages, each stage being demonstrated, imitated and practised before progressing to the next stage. After the different stages had been absorbed by the squad the complete movement was demonstrated and the whole process was practised for hours on end. At the beginning of the nineteenth century the British soldier marched with his arms held, as much as possible, as at the position of attention. The arms and hands were to be held, without stiffness, steady by his sides 'and not suffered to vibrate' when marching. He was not allowed to stoop forward, still less to lean back and his body would be kept square to the front and thrown 'rather more forward in marching than when halted.' The toe was to be a little pointed and kept near the ground, so that the shoe soles might not be visible to a person viewing from the front. When the front foot was brought to the ground it would not be drawn back but placed firmly on the ground, from toe to heel.

All marching, the side step excepted, invariably began with the left foot. The length of each pace from heel to heel was thirty inches and the recruit was to be taught to take 75 of these steps a minute 'without tottering' and with perfect steadiness. Recruits would be instructed that the pace was to be maintained for a long period of time, both in line and in column and on rough as well as smooth ground. This 'Ordinary Step' was the slowest step a recruit was taught and was also used in all movements on the parade ground.

The march in Quick Time consisted of 108 steps in the minute, each of thirty inches. On the command 'Quick - March!' the foot was to be lifted off the ground, 'that it might clear any stones or other impediments in the way and to be thrown forward and placed firm; the whole of the sole to touch the ground and not the heel alone; the knees were not to be bent, neither were they to be stiffened, so as to occasion fatigue or constraint. In Quick Time the arms might make a small motion but were not to swing out.'

The Quickest Time or Wheeling March was 120 steps in a minute, when bodies of troops were completing wheeling movements. On these occasions the outward files, having the longest distance to cover, would increase the length of their step to 33 inches.

In the same (1803) manual of instruction it was conceded that on a route march men would not be able to continue marching in the regular cadence of 75 paces of thirty inches for any considerable length of time, although it was essential that the arrival of a column at a given point was to be perfectly punctual. In the event, it was laid down that, the distance to be covered being known, a well-drilled sergeant should march at the head of the column, in the exact cadence of time; he might be relieved every half-hour by another equally well-drilled sergeant or corporal, and the commanding officer might occasionally, if considered necessary, regulate the pace by glancing at his watch. Should this method be used, the attention of the rest of the column was allowed to be relaxed, the soldiers marching on without the restraint of the cadence of step, arms could be carried, rear ranks opened to one or two paces and the files could be loosened, but never mixed up.

In the last decade of the eighteenth century and the first of the nineteenth century, in a well run battalion of the British Army, there would appear to have been little excuse for a private soldier not knowing what was required of him on the square. William Cobbett (1763-1835), the famous writer, enlisted as a young man and recorded the details of his recruit training programme at the regimental depot:

Reveille	5 a.m.
Drill	6-7.45 a.m.
Breakfast	8-9.45 a.m.
Drill	10-12.45 p.m.
Dinner	1-1.45 p.m.
Drill	2-4 p.m.

After surviving such a regime (in this case, six and a half hours of foot drill, marching skills and weapon handling, daily) a soldier would have been adjudged fit to participate in the manoeuvres of large units in the field.

At this time much importance was paid to the knowledge and practice of 'The Eighteen Manoeuvres.' The explanation of each movement was lengthy and detailed and although each and every officer should have known them perfectly, the youngest soldier was expected to have some knowledge, however sketchy, of what was required of him. If he erred and was noticed he would have been elbowed and jostled into his right place by his comrades in nearby ranks and files or, worse, knocked into position by a prod from his sergeant's spontoon or half-pike. Briefly, the manoeuvres consisted of forming Close Column on a Rear, Front or Central Position; Changing position in Open Column; Wings Thrown Back; Countermarching and Change of Position; Counter-marching by Files on the Centre of the Battalion; Marching in Open Column; Echelon Change of Position (two directions); Changing Position; Retreating in Line; Marching to a Flank in Echelon; Forming Hollow Square and its Movements; Retiring and Filing to the Rear; Filing, Advancing and Charging to the Front; Retiring in Line, and Advancing in Line.

To make things more difficult for some recruits if they were transferred to another regiment, they were taught variations of the drill to which they had become accustomed in their initial training. One such young soldier described, in his memoirs, how he had been drilled by a sergeant-major who had marched with the Light Brigade to Talavera, in the Peninsular War. Instead of the usual 75 paces to the minute he was taught the quick step, invented by Sir John Moore - three paces walking, alternating with three paces running - and was told that the Light Brigade used it on the march whenever the track was suitable and that by this means they covered six miles an hour.

In 1824 an *Abstract of the Field Exercise and Evolutions of the Army* was issued 'By His Majesty's Command' from the Adjutant-General's Office, Horse Guards. The Commander-in-Chief had decided that the Abstract should be prepared for the use, information and guidance of the non-commissioned officers of the army and every sergeant of cavalry and infantry should be provided with a copy. The Rules and Instructions therein were to be strictly adhered to.

The instructors were to teach the recruits in a clear, firm and concise manner. They had to allow for 'the weak capacity of the recruit' and were advised to be patient, not vigorous, where endeavour and goodwill were displayed by the young soldier. In the first steps of foot drill and musketry instruction, the firelock, fingers and elbows, etc., were to be 'justly placed by the Instructor but as the recruits became more practised they were not to be touched but, from the example shown and the directions given, they were taught to correct themselves, when admonished.' Recruits were not to be kept too long at any particular part of their exercises, to tire them 'or make them uneasy.' Neither fife nor music, on any account, would be used in marching practice,

> it being essential to confirm the recruit by habit alone in that cadence of step which he is afterwards to maintain in his march to the enemy, amidst every variety of noise and circumstance that may tend to derange him.

The Introduction concludes;

> In the manner hereinafter described, each recruit must be trained singly, and in squad; and, until he is perfect in all points of his duty, he is not to join the battalion - for one awkward man, imperfect in his march, or distorted in his person, will derange his division, and, of course, operate on the battalion and line in a still more injurious manner. Every soldier, on his return from long absence, must be re-drilled before he is permitted to act in the ranks of his company.

In the Abstract the position of Attention was practically the same as defined in previous drill manuals but directed that when the recruit's arms were hanging near the body, the elbows had to be kept close to the side, *the hands open to the front, with the little fingers touching the seams of the trousers.* The reason for this apparently unusual position of the elbows and hands would have been for the teaching of holding the musket later to have been made easier to explain, and 'to prevent false distances when marching in line', in other words, to keep contact with one's neighbours on left and right, to prevent gaps being formed.

It was also recommended that in order to 'supple the Recruit' and give freedom to his muscles he should be exercised in the use of a wooden club, about two and a half feet in length, rounded and shaped to the hand, and of a weight in proportion to the strength of the recruit. This should be circled round his head, continuing it in its vertical position, first with the right hand and then with the left. Later, a club would be held in each hand and circled round the head alternately. The recruit would also be practised (presumably using the club) in the extended motions laid down for the Sword Exercise. It was observed that 'Too many methods cannot be used to improve the carriage of the recruit, and banish the air of the Rustic.'

The Balance Step was used to teach the recruit how to march correctly. It was practised first by bringing the left foot forward, then back, balancing upon the right foot; then, balancing on the left foot, advancing the right foot and then bringing it back. The next movement was to gain ground by the word of command 'Forward.' The whole step was then completed by the left foot then the right and so on. In addition to the Slow Step, 75 in a minute, thirty inches in length, the recruit was to be taught the Quick Step (108 steps in a minute) and the Double March (150 steps, each of 36 inches, in the minute).

The 1833 official drill manual *Field Exercise and Evolutions of the Army* contained no substantial additions or alterations to the 1824 publication but ordered that, in marching, the foot would be raised sufficiently high to clear the ground without grazing it, carried straight to the front and, without being drawn back, placed softly on the ground so as not to jerk or shake the body in the slightest degree. A certain amount of difficulty confronted those responsible for foot drill and marching skills instruction in regiments of the Federal Army during the American Civil War which broke out in 1861. One soldier, recalling his drill parades, wrote:

> And then what inimitable marching! My company was about equally divided at first between men who could keep no time at all, those who could keep some time but not much, and those who could keep a good deal of time if each were permitted to do it in his own way. In word, it took a long while for us to become strong in rhythm.

It would appear that the authorities in America at that time were satisfied with recruits being drilled en masse, instead of in small squads, as in the European armies of the period, enabling recruits' mistakes to be readily discerned and duly rectified.

Things had not improved, judging from an account of a Victory March in Washington in 1865, after the Civil War. After the men of the Potomac had marched past in good order, those of the army of General Sherman made no attempt to keep the lines closed up and well-dressed but 'each man marched to suit his own convenience.' Men carried their weapons as they pleased, whether they were at the 'Shoulder', 'Trail' or 'Right Shoulder Shift' positions. All along the line, it was reported, the men chatted, laughed and cheered, as they pleased. During the war itself commanders of the opposing armies were sometimes chagrined to have to wait for units to complete their numbers because some of the soldiers had quit their ranks to pick blackberries or chase the odd chicken or rabbit when on the march, without being checked by their officers and sergeants.[3]

---

[3] Evidence that the men had not been vigorously drilled when enlisting is provided by the fact that on many of the battlefields of the Civil War hundreds of ramrods and burst musket barrels littered the ground because the men had neglected to remove the rods after ramming down the charge and ball, before pressing the trigger.

The *Field Exercise and Evolutions of Infantry* (printed by Her Majesty's Stationery Office in 1877) made slight variations in the detail of the position of Attention inasmuch as the feet would form an angle of 45 degrees and the hands would be kept flat against the thigh, open, with thumbs to the front and close to the forefingers.

The Slow Step was still 75 paces to the minute but the Quick Step was increased to 116 paces and 165 in Double Time. In marching the arms and hands were to be kept steady by the sides and care to be taken that 'the hand does not partake of the movement of the leg.'

Recruits and trained soldiers were still expected to have a working knowledge of manoeuvring in large bodies. The Eighteen Manoeuvres of previous years had been modified, even though the titles suggest most complex evolutions. The new manoeuvres consisted of Company Wheeling or Forming from the Halt, from Column into Line; Company in Column Changing Direction; Forming Company Square; Reinforcing an Extended Line or Prolonging it to a Flank; Battalion Marching and Retiring in Line; Charging in Line; Battalion in Line passing Obstacles; Battalion in line Wheeling into Column on the March; Receiving Cavalry in Line; Battalion in Line Forming Square; Square Marching in any Direction; Brigade in Mass of Quarter Columns Wheeling into Line of Columns, and Brigade Retiring in Columns from One Flank of Battalions in Rear of the Other or from Both Flanks of Battalions in Rear of their Centres.

By 1896 the Army Drill Manual had laid down that in Quick Time the arms of the soldier would be swung to the front and rear, not higher than the waistbelt nor across the body (as is the case at present in some European armies).

Under the heading 'Discipline' in the Infantry Training Manual of 1926, it was set out that the first and quickest method of teaching discipline was close order drill. The soldier began his instruction in drill by being taught the position of Attention. This was, in itself, the key to the purpose for which drill was invented. It secured the whole attention of the man to his commander by

An advertisment from the time of the 1914-18 War, showing the equipment worn by the British soldier

requiring absolute silence, the body rigid and motionless and the man's 'eager expectation of the word of command and instant readiness to obey it.'

Good march discipline reflected *esprit de corps*. A battalion was judged - and judged itself - by conduct on the march and by the bearing and turn-out of detached parties and individuals. Officers and men in a good marching battalion had pride in themselves. In a platoon moving well, the weaker men were unconsciously helped by the stronger men as the swing of the whole unit carried them forward. 'A straggler would be made to feel that he has disgraced himself and his regiment.'

In the detail for the position of Attention the instructions were similar to those in previous books but wrists were to be kept straight, hands closed but not clenched, backs of the fingers so closed were to touch the thigh lightly, with thumbs to the front and close to the forefingers and thumbs immediately behind the seam of the trousers.

In Slow Time 70 paces would be taken in one minute, 120 in Quick Time and 180 in Double Time. On ceremonial and drill parades, Rifle Regiments and Light Infantry, when not brigaded with other troops, marched at the rate of 140 paces a minute.

In Slow Time the soldier's arms and hands would be kept steady by his sides but in Quick Time his arms, kept as straight as their natural bend would allow, would swing naturally from the shoulder, so that the hands reached the height of the waist belt in front and go as far as possible to the rear. Hands would be kept closed but not clenched.

In the 1935 Manual of Elementary Drill general instructions for drilling recruits included the statement that slovenly drill was harmful and all movements on parade would be performed smartly. The warning that 'Noisy stamping of the feet in such movements as Turning, coming to the position of Attention, or Standing at Ease, is forbidden' was cheerfully disregarded by drill instructors at the Guards' Depot and at most of the Regimental Infantry Depots elsewhere, where recruits were (and still are) urged to do their utmost to drive their feet through the surface of the parade ground whenever these particular movements were being practised.

In 1941 an attempt was made to introduce a kind of 'Battle Drill' into the training of the British Army. The armchair experts in the War Office and some Infantry Training Centres, unable to account for the reverses of the Army up to that date, drew up a programme of drill to be learned on the parade square and perfected in the countryside. It was an attempt to break down elementary battlefield tactics into a series of simple movements and orders, so, it was presumed, that the soldier's responses on a real battlefield would become as automatic as movements learned on the parade ground.

The standing 'Right Flanking' or 'Left Flanking' attack, according to the drill, involved one party marching round to one side, turning right or left, hurling imaginary grenades and finally doubling forward on the command 'Go in with the bayonet!' while another section, playing the role of providing covering fire whilst lying in prone positions on the ground, would shout, at the crucial moment 'cease covering fire!' On another occasion, whilst marching in single file along the side of a road, one soldier would call out 'I am watching for an enemy to my front', others would indicate that they were watching the left or right flanks whilst the men bringing up the rear would duly report on the vigilance being paid to the rear.

Battle Drill as a training programme did not survive very long as more and more people came to realise what a ridiculous time-wasting charade this all was, worthy of an episode of a 'Dad's Army' television series to be shown a generation later.

The 1967 *Army Drill Book* laid down that the Quick March would normally be at the rate of 116 paces to the minute although recruits would start their training by marching at up to 140 paces to the minute 'to encourage agility and alertness.' The Slow March would be carried out at 65 paces to the minute and would be used primarily on ceremonial occasions. Throughout the Army, units had their traditional rates of quick marching, which they could use unless several units, who had different rates of marching, were on the same parade, when all would march at 116 paces to the minute, except Light Infantry and Green Jacket Regiments, who would march past at 140 paces to the minute if practicable. On mixed ceremonial parades, Light Infantry Regiments would be prepared to forego their position of seniority and march past last at the regulation Light Infantry pace.

In the instructions for the Quick March it was laid down that the forward heel would strike the ground first, with the knee braced back on impact. The arms would be swung freely until the bottom of the hand was in line with the top of the waistbelt and backwards as far as they would go. Recruits would be taught to swing the arm forward so that the top of the hand was in line with the top of the breast pocket. Each man in a squad was responsible for keeping his own dressing and the correct step. The leading man of the guiding flank of a squad would dictate their direction, length of pace and rate of marching.

In the current drill manual of the Royal Marines, not only is it emphasised that in teaching recruits how to march the heel should come to the ground first, but in the common faults to be checked the instructors will be on the alert for, amongst other points, on the first pace of the Quick March, the left foot would not be placed flat on the ground nor the knee bent too much.

In the instructions for the Slow March the 1967 Army *Drill Book* described how the little toe of the left foot was to touch the ground first whilst the Royal Marines instruction was for the toes to be placed on the ground before the heel, the outer edge of the sole of the boot going to the ground first. The movements are similar in many respects to the step of the men of the armies of Marlborough and Frederick the Great as they marched across Europe at their normal pace.[4]

At the present time preparations are being made to introduce a new Foot and Arms Drill Book for the British Army and from information available it would appear that there will be little change in the patterns of marching or the method of teaching them for the British infantryman. The description of 'forcing' or 'driving' the foot to the ground seems to legalize the 'Noisy Stamping of the Feet' frowned upon in the 1935 *Manual of Elementary Drill*.

For the past few years a system of assessing the standard of personal fitness for troops in the British Army has been in

---

[4] As an illustration of how customs change over the years, the author was taught that the foot movement in the Slow March was to 'Kick the foot forward then glide, before placing it flat on the ground.' (Guards' Depot in November 1939).

operation. Tests are graded according to age and some age groups have a choice of alternative types of test. Briefly, a Basic Fitness Test (BFT) consists of running and marching a certain distance in a squad or individually, on level ground, wearing trousers and athletic vest. Time limits are set, depending upon the ages of the participants. The tests are to be taken at least twice yearly.

To ensure that all members of the Field Army are physically capable of carrying out their combat roles, Combat Fitness Tests (CFT) must be performed satisfactorily. Those failing a second time are subjected to a course of remedial fitness training under the supervision of an Army Physical Training Corps instructor. One of the tests is to march a distance of eight miles (12.87 kilometres) in Complete Equipment Fighting Order (CEFO), carrying 30-35lbs (13.5-15.8 kgs), (including personal weapon). Helmets can be worn for all or part of the test, at the Commanding Officer's discretion. The Director of Infantry may order an increase in battle load for infantry units to 44lbs (19.9 kgs). Three miles of this march has to be across country terrain and the march completed in a formed body. The test has to be accomplished in one hour and fifty minutes or less. An alternative test is to complete three miles (4.8 km) within 33 minutes, dressed and carrying the same weight as before. The course has to be on level ground affording a good running surface.

Part II of the Combat Fitness Test consists of clearing a ditch five feet (1.5 metres) wide whilst wearing CEFO and carrying weapon; mount and dismount a 4-ton truck with its tail-board up, wearing the same equipment, and lift and carry for ninety metres in a 'fireman's lift' a man of similar body weight. In the latter section both men carry weapons but wear no equipment.

In an Army booklet on endurance training it is stated that route marching is not a time-cost-effective method of improving stamina if the march is of less than three hours. However, the booklet goes on, 'if a distance of 40 kilometres (25 miles) over varied ground is covered in about seven hours, a soldier's confidence will be enhanced and the distance does have a training effect even though the same effect could have been achieved in much less time by running a much shorter distance.'

Although it is said to be a symptom of advancing years should an old soldier proclaim that 'they don't breed 'em as tough as they used to!' a hard, sweaty run over a shorter distance is infinitely more preferable to the old-fashioned 25-30 mile hard-slogging route march, mile after mile of never-ending road and stinging sweat. It has been estimated recently that some of the British infantry during the cruel Peninsular campaign had fought and marched over 6,000 miles, in extremes of temperatures and across the most difficult terrain, in uncomfortable uniforms, carrying heavy loads and wearing shoes of poor quality. Compare the experiences of these men with those who participated in the Falklands Campaign of 1982 and were asked to march not more than sixty miles over open country, across rocky or boggy ground. Many were the complaints of water seeping into their boots, causing 'trench foot' and blisters caused by allegedly unsuitable footwear. It is possible that much of the trouble would have been averted by more suitable training and adequate instruction in the principles of foot hygiene.

The Parachute Regiment seems to have grasped the inadequacies of the Basic Fitness and Combat Fitness Tests and has introduced two further tests - the '10-miler' (16 kilometres), carrying a total of 44lbs (19.8 kgs), including Bergen rucksack, helmet and webbing, to be completed in one hour 45 minutes, and the '2-miler', carrying 35lbs in webbing equipment and wearing combat kit, including weapon and helmet, to be completed in 18 minutes.

Soldiers wishing to volunteer for the Special Air Service (SAS) undergo the first of three weeks of an Aptitude Test, consisting of navigation and fitness training then have to endure a fourth week, known as Test Week. They have to complete five marches, each of 20-30 kilometres, carrying a Bergen of 40-55lbs and a rifle, at an average speed of about five kilometres an hour. The week culminates in an endurance march of 65 kilometres, carrying 55lbs and a rifle. This must be completed within 20-24 hours, depending on conditions.

(Soldiers who successfully complete Test Week go on to continuation training, lasting thirteen weeks, including skill at arms, range firing, medical and demolition training and the Army Combat Survival Instructors' Course. On completion of continuation training those already parachute trained go to SAS Squadrons; those not so trained go for a basic course.)

The Royal Marine Commando Training Wing has inaugurated a new system of training designed to increase the fitness of recruits, yet adopting a more caring 'softly, softly' approach to the men. Training, although more vigorous, is made more enjoyable, given the hardships recruits must undergo to prepare for the rigours of the battlefield. The 'pat on the back' is now seen more often than the previous eyeball-to-eyeball confrontation between a purple-faced instructor and quaking young marines.

Despite the more relaxed approach recruits still have to complete a nine-mile speed march in ninety minutes, the endurance course in 71 minutes, the 'Tarzan' course in thirteen minutes, and the 30 mile march across Dartmoor with 30lbs of kit in eight hours.

The instruction of drill and marching skills throughout the world does not vary to a significant degree and the soldiers of one army could accustom themselves to the requirements of instructors in other lands without too much difficulty. What will vary, however, is the energy and drive displayed by the individual instructors and the liveliness and dedication of those carrying out the particular orders.

The position of Attention for soldiers of the army of the United States is markedly similar to that taught to the British soldier. When it comes to marching off from this position, however, a knowledgeable observer will notice a considerable difference in smartness and execution. On the command 'Forward, March!' the American steps off, keeping the head and eyes to the front, as expected. He is instructed to swing his arms in a 'natural' motion, without exaggeration and without bending at the elbows, approximately nine inches to the front and six inches straight to the rear of the trouser seams. The fingers are curled as in the position of Attention so that the fingers just clear the trousers. This apparent restriction of the natural swing of the arms, repeated through a whole squad, platoon or company, gives an unfortunate impression of sloppiness in movement, compared to the more spirited swing of the arms in other armies. The situation is worsened when the command 'At Ease, March!' is given as either foot strikes the ground. The soldier is then no longer required to march in step, although his approximate interval and distance are maintained in his formation. He is not allowed to talk. The Route Step March is executed exactly the same as At Ease March except that the soldier may drink from his canteen and talk.

In the French Army the position of Attention is adopted with the heels together and in line, the arms hanging downwards close to the body and the palms flat against the thighs and the fingers extended. On a route march the soldiers on the order 'Pas de Route, Marche' are allowed to talk, sing and smoke. When ordered 'Pas sans Cadence' they need not keep step with their comrades but are not allowed to talk or smoke.

The position of Attention in the Soviet Army is similar to that in Britain, save that the palms are half bent and held against the thighs. The Standing at Ease position is reached by relaxing the right knee and leg or left knee and leg, without moving the position of the feet. Talking is not permitted. The normal marching pace is 110-120 steps per minute, the running pace increasing to 165-180 steps per minute.

There are two marching movements. The Formation Step[5] commences with leg and toes stretched out forward with the foot 15-20 centimetres from the ground and placed down firmly, followed by the other foot and leg. The elbows are bent so that they are brought forward above the belt buckle, then brought backwards as far as the shoulder joints will allow, keeping the fingers half-bent. The Campaign Step calls for a normal marching action, with arms moving freely round the body. In the West German Army, on the command 'March in Step' the soldier steps out with his left foot and marches at 114 steps to the minute. He moves his arms with his hands open and fingers extended but free and easy to about a hand's breadth below the waistbelt. Singing on

---

[5] Known to the British as the Goose Step, the custom is believed to have originated in Russia and adopted by the Prussian Army in the 18th century.

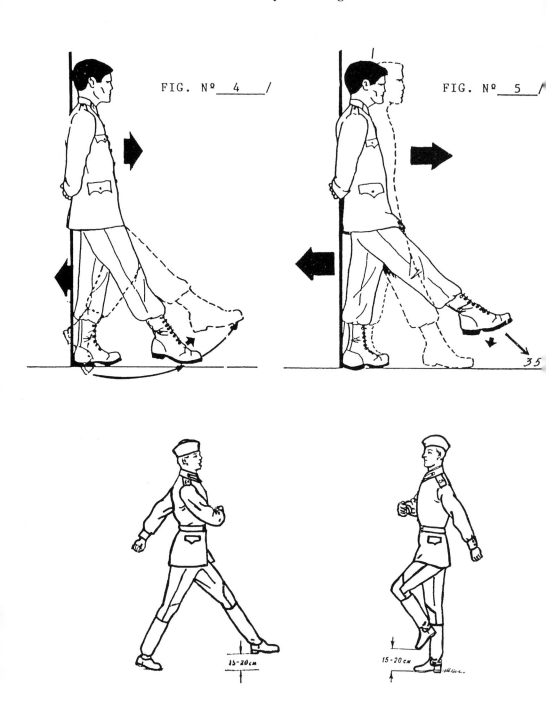

FIG. Nº 4

FIG. Nº 5

35

15-20 cm

15-20 cm

Illustrations from the Soviet Army and Chilean Army drill books about the parade or formation step and marching on the spot the march is meticulously set out in the drill manual. On the command of the unit leader 'At Ease - A Song', the first rank decides on a known marching song and the right-hand man calls out in a loud voice the title. The men behind him pass on the title to those behind them until the men in the rear rank receive the message. Their right-hand man calls out 'The song is through!'. The front rank sing the first note of the song, the unit takes up the note, whereupon the right-hand man of the front rank counts out loud 'One, two', the first two ranks count 'three, four' as they put down their left feet and the whole unit begins to sing the song chosen as they put down their left feet. On the command from the leader 'Stop Singing' the unit obeys. When on a route march and Marching Easy the British infantry start singing whenever a lone voice sings out the first note or two of a popular song or any soldier with a mouth organ plays a bar or two. Singing stops when the command 'March at Ease' is given by their commander. (The Army authorities seem to have been health-conscious for over a century now as for that period of time soldiers were allowed to smoke their pipes on a route march but never cigarettes or cigars.)

In the West German Army the Parade (or 'Goose') Step is no longer used because, it is said, of its unhappy connections with the former Reichswehr. In the East German People's Army, however, the Parade Step and its derivations, popular for a time in countries of Eastern Europe under Soviet influence, and elsewhere, is still being used. Recent events have caused a re-think in this matter and there is a possibility that steps will be taken to scrap the long and tedious ritual of goose-stepping military parades. In Chile the Goose-step is taught because 'it is a fairly difficult exercise that demands of all soldiers energy, precision and perfection in its execution.' When the order 'Troops Ceremonial Pace, March' is given to troops of the Turkish Army, they march off at the rate of 114 steps to the minute, the knees not being bent and the soles of the boots not made visible to the front. The fingers are clenched and the arms swung level with the shoulder.

In Greece the Ceremonial March of units such as the Ezvones, with their picturesque uniforms, is unique. The step, from way back in history, consists of the knees being raised much higher than normal, with the arms raised higher than the shoulders, and involves turns in an intricate pattern.

Thanks to the increased television coverage of events all over the world it is sometime possible to compare the marching styles of troops in other countries. For sheer military precision and after lengthy weeks of practice, the massed goose-stepping parades of the armies of the People's Republic of China and the Soviet Union must take precedence but the more relaxed and workmanlike marching style of British, German and South African infantry, whether they be on ceremonial parade or on route marches, would appear to set high standards. When marching normally, using the Campaign Step, the Soviet soldier is every bit as pleasing to watch as his counterparts in the three countries mentioned above and, in addition, judging by his carriage and freely moving arms, he seems to enjoy the experience of moving in an easier style than the stiff Formation Step.

Despite the advent of the armoured personnel carrier and the troop-carrying helicopter, the basic training principle of nearly all modern armies is to turn the recruit into a good marksman and a vigorous marcher. At one time war was considered to be mainly a question of legs. Victory on the battlefield, generally speaking, went to the commander who made the best use of the rapid mobility and precision in movement of his infantry.

Maurice, Comte de Saxe (1696-1750) was one of the architects of infantry manoeuvre in the eighteenth century. A Marshal of France, he had served under Prince Eugene in the Netherlands and under Peter the Great of Russia against the Swedes. He once said that

> The main part of the exercise of war regards the legs and not the arms; in the legs lies all the secret of manoeuvres and combats, and it is with the legs that the principal pains should be taken. Whoever acts differently is a dolt, and has not mastered the elements of what goes by the name of the art of war.

Chapter Five

Marching Aids

In the armies of ancient times the method of teaching young soldiers how to march correctly and in step was probably by showing them what the instructor wanted them to do then getting them to imitate what they had just seen. After centuries of using different aids this system is still basically followed by the best drill instructors.

In the Guards' Depot the recruits are still ordered to watch while the instructor shows them what happens after the order 'Quick - March!' is given. After a few paces the instructor orders himself to 'Halt!' The movements are then broken into parts and each part, in sequence, is demonstrated, imitated by each member of the squad and faults pointed out. After one part has been mastered, the next part is demonstrated and so on, until the complete movement has been learned. The parts are then put together, running from 'Quick - March' to 'Halt', demonstrated by the instructor then practised by the squad, checked by the instructor and his assistant(s).

In the days when the length of a man's step was considered a matter of life and death on the battlefield and the difference between victory and defeat, extraordinary methods were devised to ensure that the correct length of stride was being taken. A British drill book of 1803, for example, recommended that in order to acquire an exact length of pace, cords, the thickness of a jack-line, should be prepared by tying small pieces of red cloth on them, at a distance of 30 inches (the length of a pace); at the end of 75 paces (the number of steps in Ordinary Time) or ties, a piece of cloth larger than the rest was to be fastened; at 108 paces (Quick Time) a piece of cloth of a different colour again, to mark the extent of the Quickest Time of 120 paces. Two of the cords were to be stretched parallel and distant one from the other, the extent of the front destined for the march not exceeding 15 or 20 files.

If the march was to be in Ordinary Time, a man or a camp colour could be placed at the end of 75 paces. When the rank or division was correctly dressed, the instructor, with a stop watch in his hand, would give the order to march, and the instant the minute expired he would order 'Halt!' and by this means he could perceive at once whether the march had been too fast or too slow.

Care would always be taken that the men stepped their full pace of 30 inches and that the flanks of the body marching arrived at the extremity of the cords by an equal number of steps corresponding with the marks. If a quicker pace was required it would only be necessary to remove the camp colour or other marker on each flank to the marks at 108 or 120 and proceed as directed. If one of the cords was prolonged to a considerable distance the men might be made to march for one or several minutes together in Quick or Ordinary Time.

With this system being followed it was suggested that squads of officers, sergeants, drummers and musicians should be practised to march and thereby acquire the correct length of pace.

Eventually the use of the cords could be dispensed with and officers and sergeants were requested to take up distances on the ground to serve as points for directing the march. Afterwards, the use of even ground should be abandoned for the open field, ploughed and stubble lands, where no cords would be required, nor sergeants to serve as points of direction, but the commander was advised to fix a bush, a tree or some other distant object, as the point on which to march.

To ensure the correct timing of paces to the minute, a plummet, made from a musket ball, suspended by a string of whipcord, on which were marked the different required lengths, had to be in the possession of each squad instructor (and also the drummajor) and constantly referred to to correct 'uncertainty of movement' by the soldiers marching. The different lengths of plummets, swinging the times of the different marches in a minute, were as follows:

Time	Inches	Hundredth	Parts
Ordinary Time	(75 paces to the minute)	24	96
Quick Time	(108 paces do.)	12	3
Quickest Time	(120 paces do.)	9	80

The length of the plummet line was to be measured from the point of suspension to the centre of the ball.

The use of plummets was made mandatory in the official drill book of 1824, with an additional step, the Double March, being checked by a plummet of the length of 6 inches and 20 hundredths. Accurate distances of steps were also to be marked out on the ground, along which the soldier would be practised to march and thereby acquire the correct length of pace.

In a drill book of 1877 it was laid down that no recruit or squad of soldiers would be taught to march without the use of the drum and pace stick and, to check whether the time was beaten correctly, a pendulum or plummet had to be used.

The exact time of the advent of the pace-stick in the British Army and whether it was introduced from the Continent has been the subject of much argument in military circles. Drill sergeants in Europe have used a form of stick since the 18th century and possibly earlier. The simple version could be used as a pointer, a device for pushing men into line (like the spontoon or halberd), an instrument for administering punishment and as a symbol of rank or authority. In some quarters it is thought that a kind of pace-stick or a similar instrument was once used by gunners to space their pieces correctly on the gun-line but this opinion is repudiated by the Royal Artillery Institution who have stated that the distance between guns played no part in the external ballistic calculations of the gunnery of the 18th and 19th centuries and, therefore, there was no reason to space the guns and no need for a pace-stick to check the distance between them.

The pattern for the present-day pace-stick may have been devised by an ingenious drill instructor who recognised that a stick, if split longitudinally and hinged would form a compass-like inverted 'V' shape when opened out and would be useful for checking the length of a pace.[1] The hinge of a modern pace-stick is usually about 10 centimetres below the top of the head and the stick keeps this shape by having a crossbar affixed, usually of brass and inset into the inner surface of one of the legs, which slots into an aperture in the opposite leg, forming an 'A' shape. The bottom edge of the crossbar is slotted and is positioned near the apex so that the distance between the tips can be regulated by choosing a particular slot. A spring clip retains the crossbar and prevents it from slipping when in use. When the pace-stick is closed, a similar spring clip near the ferrule locks with a projecting ring.

As well as checking the length of a soldier's stride, the stick is used to measure a given number of steps or frontage so that parades and drill formation can be accurately worked out.

It is usually held in the palm of the right hand with the 'leading leg' of the stick perpendicular, the ferrule resting on the ground. The user pivots the other point around with a flick of the wrist and brings it to rest in the same direction of the march whilst at the same time taking one step forward the same length as the distance between the two points. One example of a pace-stick has distance settings for 12, 15, 21, 31, 33, 36 and 40 inches. A 12-inch setting can be used to check the distance between a soldier's heels when Standing at Ease, fifteen is for the length of the Side Step, thirty for standard pace, thirty-three for Stepping Out and so on. More recent sticks have settings for 27-inches, which is the length of pace of the Women's Royal Army Corps.

In 1926 the *Infantry Training Manual* prescribed that recruits were not to be taught to march without the constant use

---

[1] Similarly, a drill stick was devised by the Regimental Sergeant major of the 6th Airborne Division Training Centre at Petah Tiqva in Palestine in 1946. The length of the head of the stick, made of copper, was the exact width of a soldier's khaki drill shirt sleeve turn-up; the ferrule, of the same metal, was the measurement of the width of a hose-top turn-down. The stick was made in the Centre workshop. Robert Blakeney, in his *A Boy in the Peninsular War*, described how, as a Captain, he was drilled by a dress sergeant on the drill square in Mullingar (Westmeath, Ireland), armed with 'a colossal pair of widely yawning compasses to measure the length of a step.' This was in 1828.

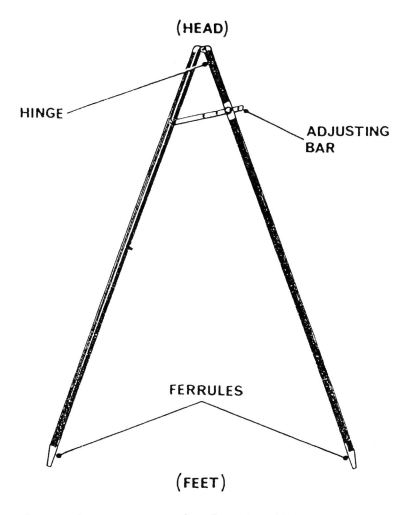

(HEAD)

HINGE

ADJUSTING
BAR

FERRULES

(FEET)

The British Army pace stick in 'open' position

of the drum and pace-stick. Before the squad was put in motion a drummer would beat the time in which the men were to march, the men paying special attention. The squad would then be marched off and the drummer would beat the time occasionally while the men were on the move. In order to check that the correct time was being beaten a metronome would be used. The length would be checked by means of the pace-stick, the accuracy of which would occasionally be checked by measurement.

The drill book for 1967 directed that the metronome itself should be checked frequently against a stopwatch to ensure that it was accurate. Extra information was included regarding the correct use of the pace-stick, the method of carrying it and a description of various drill movements when carrying the stick open and closed and when saluting with the stick carried under the arm.

Position of Attention with pace stick in the 'open' position.

From the time of the Ancient Greeks the sound of instruments was recognised as a means of communication and it was soon appreciated that during the noise and confusion of battle the sound of the drum seemed to be the most obvious way of signalling orders when the voice could not be heard. The beat of the drum was also found useful in gathering fighting men together for battle and, when cadenced marching became more general, keeping them in step. Later, when more melodic signals became necessary, another instrument, the trumpet, was brought into use, followed by the fife or flute.

During the Crusades the use of drums and cymbals by the Turks was noted by the European commanders and when they returned home some of them brought them into use in their armies.

Henry VII (reigned 1485-1509) is credited with bringing the military drum and fife to our shores and in the reign of his son, Henry VIII (1509-1547), 'drommers and ffyfers' led the muster of the London Trained Bands in 1539. In the army of Elizabeth I (1558-1603), drummers and fifers were considered as important as standard-bearers and were allotted certain places in the order of battle.

The Swiss, in the early part of the sixteenth century, were a military nation and provided mercenary soldiers in all parts of Europe. They marched to the sound of the drum and the Germans were not long in following them. From the Germans sprang many of the customs of the British Army, for instance, the pattern of drum-beats at the beginning of a march, before the rest of the instruments join in. When the fifes were first used in Britain they were called 'Almain [German] whistles.' (The German word *pfeife* means 'fife or whistle').

Instruments first known as hautboys (oboes) were issued to the British Horse Grenadiers in 1678 and each troop of the newly-raised regiments of dragoons was allowed an oboe and two drums. The Foot Guards and regiments of infantry of the line introduced bandsmen at the same time.

Those who have made a study of early military music do not appear to agree as to the dates on which the first bands and instruments were brought into use in Britain. The first regimental band is said to have been owned by the Royal Artillery in 1762 when special instructions concerning its pay and discipline were issued but this does not preclude the possibility that other regiments might have had their own bands and instruments, probably paid for by the officers out of their own pockets, before this date.

It is not known when the bagpipe first came to Britain. It was an ancient Greek and Roman instrument and was used by the Germans, Swedes and French long before it came to our shores but, of course, its use for marching infantry became famous in Scotland, thence North America, Canada, Australia and most of the lands where the Scots made their homes. As a result of its use in the British Army other nations, such as the Indians, Pakistanis and Gurkhas, adopted the pipes wholeheartedly as part of their military traditions.

At the beginning of the 18th century, the strident music of Turkish military bands, with kettle-drums and side drums, bass drums, cymbals, triangles, shawms (a type of oboe), fifes and a variety of instruments for making rhythmic sounds, attracted attention in Europe. In the second decade Poland, then Russia, obtained the services of Turkish military bands. By 1741 Austria possessed Turkish instruments and Marshal de Saxe introduced the music into his Uhlans regiments.

The huge war drums, sometimes 1.80 metres high, with diameters of 1.20 metres, used by the Turks, played on the backs of camels and, on one occasion, carried on the back of an elephant, were not used in any of the European armies but one type of musical device became popular in some countries. These took the form of a pole, with several transverse brass plates of crescent shape and sometimes terminated at the top with a conical hat-shaped object. On all these parts were suspended small bells which the player caused to jingle loudly as he marched along. The shapes on the pole varied in pattern and long tassels were sometimes attached to the extremities. The instrument became known as a Chinese Crescent or Hat.

A similar instrument, used mainly in Turkey, was a large baton called a *Çevkân*, decorated with chains and bells. As the band marched along the baton was swung to and fro in the rhythm of the march, causing the chains and bells to jingle. Instruments similar in design received the British Army nickname of 'Jingling Johnnies'. It is possible that the later German *Glockenspiel* ('Chime of Bells') was derived from the Turkish pattern. The name covers a variety of instruments carried in a military band. Some consist of a series of bells or tuned metal rods, sometimes enclosed in a lyre-shaped crescent on a pole, or a number of inverted metal cups arranged pyramid fashion on a support held in the hand. Whatever the shape of the instrument used it is played like a xylophone by striking the bells or rods with a small hammer and accentuates the rhythm played by the band.

Turkish players were never engaged in British Army bands as they were never in Europe but negroes were enlisted to play the Turkish instruments, although 'blackamoors' had been employed in the army as side-drummers, kettle-drummers and trumpeters for quite half a century before, clad in exotic uniforms. These took the form of gaudy coats and elaborate turbans in extravagant Eastern style. Their antics became a feature in military marching, of which the leopard or tiger-skin aprons of the drummers and the complicated drumstick drill of today are relics.

Despite the inclusion of music and drums in the British Army, to assist the marching tempo, in common with their Prussian counterparts, infantry were taught to ignore the drumbeat if it were sounded wrongly. In the 1803 drill book, for example, the use of music and drums was expressly forbidden to regulate the march in movement or manoeuvre. It was stated that the musicians 'never persevere in ordered time or in any other; are constantly changing measure; create noise; derange the equality of step and counteract the very end they are supposed to promote.' It went on to state that 'the ordered and cadenced march can be acquired and served from the eye and habit alone and troops must, by great practice, be so steadied as to be able to maintain it, even though drums or music of any kind should mark a different time.'

The instruction was repeated in the *Field Exercise Manual* of 1833 in that neither fife nor music would on any account be used in the instruction of drill. The recruit was to learn by practice to maintain the cadence of step 'amidst every variety of noise and circumstance that may tend to derange him.'

The advice to 'Ignore the drumbeat' had been a principle long held in the Prussian Army. Although it had a generous allowance of drummers and fifers (about fifteen per battalion) who beat out commands in the field and sounded 'Tattoo' every evening as a signal to the men to clear the inns and sutlers' tents and return to their quarters, the army did not need musicians to mark the pace of their marching. They were proud to be able to keep step without the fife and drum and for most of the time they marched and paraded in perfect silence except for the crash of the feet on the ground.

As the number of instruments in military bands increased and their variety allowed greater scope in the type and depth of the melodic ensemble able to be played, standardisation began to take a larger part in the musical arrangements. The Germans, once again, were the pioneers, followed by the British and French armies. As the standards of excellence continually rose, inevitably the repertoire of military bands widened - the playing of military marches, the raison d'être for the formation of regimental bands, gave way to extracts from operatic and classical music. Worse, United States Army bands, playing the latest 'hit' tunes, are in the habit of gyrating within their ranks as they perform - and can no longer be regarded as 'marching aids' to their infantry.

In addition to providing the primary object of military music - to ensure a definite rhythm for marching - the themes of pieces sometimes reflect the national temperament of the time of their composition. The Prussian Army and its successors marched to the stirring music of *Der Hohenfriedberger* and *Der Torgauer Marsch*, written to commemorate the victories of Frederick the Great's armies in 1745 and 1760 or *Alte Kamaraden* in memory of old army comrades. The French Army had its favourites from the time of the Napoleonic Wars, of which *Ça Ira* was the most popular.

The British Army's choice of regimental marches and similar pieces seems to be wide and varied. They range through a variety of emotions and experiences - love songs, conviviality, hunting and poaching themes, victory in battle, whims of military men and their womenfolk and thoughts about nature and the countryside. Tunes by great composers and obscure musicians have been purloined and liberties have been taken with material composed for quite a different and more innocent purpose; solemn hymn tunes have been turned into marching songs with sometimes coarse, even obscene, lyrics. Some of the music has been played for centuries - *Dumbarton's Drums*, the regimental march of the Royal Scots, has been heard for over three hundred years. Marches played by the country's enemies have been taken over by British regiments - *Ça Ira* ('That will be swept away') was being sung in 1793 by French troops in Flanders when the British 14th Foot was being repulsed. The commanding officer of the 14th (later the Prince of Wales's Own Regiment of Yorkshire) ordered the drums to strike up the same music, with the words 'We'll beat them to their own damn tune!' The 14th rallied and drove the French from the field. In the Second World War British and German infantry marched while singing the same songs - *Roll out the Barrel* and *Lilli Marlene*.

Some British regiments have two or three pieces of music incorporated in their regimental marches and the full list must number nearly two hundred. Examples of the titles seem to reflect the lively, even jaunty, style of marching by the infantry in days gone by, when troops travelled nearly everywhere on foot:

The Rising of the Lark (Welsh Guards)
Corn Rigs are Bonny (King's Own Royal Regiment - Lancaster)
Here's to the Maiden of Bashful Fifteen (King's Regiment - Liverpool)
The Lincolnshire Poacher (Lincolnshire Regiment)
Speed the Plough (Suffolk Regiment)
The Bonnie English Rose (Green Howards)
The Kynegad Slashers (Gloucestershire Regiment)
Come, Lasses and Lads (South Staffordshire Regiment)

The Dashing White Sergeant (Royal Berkshire Regiment)
The Young May Moon (Sherwood Foresters)
Old Soldiers Never Die (Middlesex Regiment)

Before the advent of the military band soldiers marched and sang to the sound of the drum and fife or, later, the tin whistle and mouth organ. Cromwell's soldiers marched, lustily singing hymns on the march - the men of the First World War sang to the same music but with different verses. Without doubt, the most popular and lively marching song used by the British soldier over the longest period of time was 'The Girl I Left Behind Me'. It was first used about 1758 and the first verse suggests that although he may have been a rough fellow on the outside, the Redcoat was a sentimental soul at heart:

> 'I'm lonesome since I crossed the hill,
> And o'er the moor and valley,
> Such grievous thoughts my heart do fill,
> Since parting with my Sally.
> I seek no more the fine or gay,
> For each does but remind me,
> How swift the hours did pass away,
> With the girl I've left behind me.'

The First World War was notable for many popular marching songs. Besides music-hall favourites like *Tipperary, Pack up your Troubles in your old Kitbag*, and *There's a Long, Long Trail a-winding*, the sauciest, downright disgraceful ditties were those sung to well-known hymn and Salvation Army tunes. *We are Fred Karno's Army, Wash me in the Water that you washed your Dirty Daughter, When this Bloody* [or worse] *War is Over, Jesus wants me for a Sunbeam* and *I Don't want to be a Soldier* are just a few of those bellowed on the march.

The marching songs of the Second World War were not so memorable. The days when troops could march along roads for miles in files of three or four were practically over. In the first year or two *Bless 'Em All, I've got a Lovely Bunch of Coconuts* and *Our*

Sergeant Major, He's one of the Forty Thieves (and the Colour Bloke's the other thirty-nine), sung to the tune of *John Brown's Body*, together with songs or parodies heard on the wireless, seem to have been some of the most popular. Gradually, as the war became more intense and masses of troops on the march became more vulnerable, troops did not march in large bodies any more but moved in single file along the sides of the road or across country.

During this period, whilst it was noted that the British and German troops generally appeared to keep step on the roads, the Soviet Army did not always do so. The American soldier, on the other hand, did not seem to relish the experience of marching long distances at all, still less to keep in step whilst doing so.

Although the German Army method of singing on the march and the drill required to get it going seems troublesome, the end-product is invariably harmonious and enjoyable to the troops and listeners alike. Favourites such as *Schwartz-braun ist die Haselnuss* ('Dark brown is the hazel-nut') and *O du Westerwald* ('Oh, you beautiful Westerwald'), when sung in unison, accompanied by the sound of marching boots, is a memorable experience. Sadly, in one sense, if the current trend in waging war continues, with troops moving forward enclosed in armoured hulls, the spectacle and sound of marching infantry will fade away into history.

Glockenspiel presented by Queen Victoria in 1846 to the band of the Royal Marines at Portsmouth.

Chapter Six

Clothing and Equipment of the Marching Soldier.

From the beginning of wars experiments have been carried out to determine the most efficient and comfortable means of getting armed men to the battlefield. The first warriors probably made do with their weapons and animal skins fashioned into items of clothing. If the journey to be undertaken was a lengthy one food and other necessaries would be carried in bags or slung over the shoulder by means of thongs.

In the course of time those undertaking long journeys in poor weather conditions and across rough terrain would have furnished themselves with pieces of animal hide fastened to the feet by thongs around the ankle, to protect their feet. Later came moccasins made of leather fastened together with rawhide laces. Sandals came next, with a variety of fastenings and the final military sandal of the Roman soldier was a simple version of the British Army ammunition boot of the late nineteenth century right up to the 1950s, with leather uppers and hobnails.

At the beginning of the English Civil War in 1642 the foot soldiers on both sides normally wore their own comfortable clothing and footwear and carried their food, ammunition and other necessaries in cloth bags slung over their shoulders or in their pockets. They were issued with a variety of weapons acquired from parish stocks, landowners' stores and so on. The more simple weapons like pikes and swords could be made by competent blacksmiths and more sophisticated weapons like firearms could be issued by commanders who had acquired them by purchase or requisition. Illustrations showing the Cavaliers wearing large-brimmed hats with curling feathers and foppish clothing, and the Roundheads with lobster-tailed helmets, protective face-pieces, buff tunics and, sometimes, breastplates, are wide of the mark; the reality is that during the early part of the war both sides wore similar clothing and carried similar arms and equipment. It would have been difficult for an observer to have differentiated between Royalist and Parliamentary troops on the march.

Well into the eighteenth century the foot soldier marched into action with simple footwear not unlike that which he had worn in civilian life. Marlborough's infantry, for example, on their famous march to the Danube in 1704, wore high buckled shoes. They would have suffered the usual discomfort of men on the march because of the equipment strapped round their bodies. They wore the military dress of the time - tricorn hats, red coats, breeches and gaiters and wore cross-belts, swords, bayonets, knapsacks, 24 cartridges each in pockets, and carried heavy flintlock muskets, cooking pots, food, washing kit and cloaks. The weight carried by each man would have totalled 50lbs (22.5 kgs). In addition, the sergeants would have carried heavy half-pikes or spontoons and pikemen would have carried a much longer and heavier weapon.

The shoes of the Prussian soldier in the time of Frederick the Great were made of good leather, black in colour and in the characteristically Prussian style with square toes and fairly high heels. It was said that the shoes and gaiters served to hide the appalling smell of the sweaty woollen stockings underneath. Worse, some soldiers used to cut off the bottoms of the stockings altogether[1] and wrapped the feet in strips of cloth which were impregnated with tallow to make them softer. It was said at the time that the stench of a Prussian column on the march was powerful enough to linger in the air on a still day for minutes after the troops had passed.

From the time of Frederick the Great more care was exercised in making the uniforms and equipment attractive to look at than comfortable for the wearers. The Prussian Army uniform varied - the hats worn by the infantry came in three styles: the tall brass-fronted mitre caps of the grenadiers, the similar but lower cap

---

[1] Hosetops were worn by the British soldier with the hot weather uniform of khaki drill shorts and shirts from the early part of the twentieth century until recently. Ordinary short woollen socks were worn on the feet and the 'join' between the top of the socks and the bottom of the hosetops was covered by short puttees or gaiters.

of the fusiliers and the three-cornered hat of the veteran regiments
of the line. Under the infantry coat was a waistcoat, a linen dickey
and a coarse shirt. The breeches were of rough wool and gaiters
were of ticking, linen or ordinary cloth, closed down the sides by
a row of small buttons and secured below the knee by a band.

A broad bandolier of whitened leather was slung over the
left shoulder and held a cartridge pouch behind the right hip. The
pouch was a large box of thick leather. It contained a leather bag
with an inner box or cartouche for about eighty cartridges. A tin
water flask was slung by a narrow leather strap over the right
shoulder. The men took turns in carrying a large field kettle issued
to each tent-section. The knapsack was a bag of calfskin worn on
the left side of the back, just behind the sword, hanging from
another narrow leather strap slung over the right shoulder.

In the knapsack was carried a spare dickey, shirts, gaiter
buttons, breeches, hose, foot bands and flints, as well as gloves,
bandage and tourniquet, under-cuffs, hair powder, knife, fork and
spoon, salt, mirror, brushes, combs, wax for the shoes and
cartridge pouch, buff leather polisher, gaiter hook, screwdriver, gun
oil and ramrod worm. As if this load were not sufficient, three tent
pegs were tied to the supporting strap and a linen bread bag was
suspended on its own little strap just below the knapsack. To
complete the ensemble, the sword belt was buckled around the
man's middle and lay immediately on top of the waistcoat.
Hanging on the sword belt near the sword was the narrow
triangular-sectioned bayonet in a scabbard.

The Prussian soldier also had to work hard to maintain his
smart appearance and the condition of his clothing and equipment.
Every time he came off parade and after a march he had to polish
his musket to mirror brightness with a thick piece of buckskin,
and the wood of the stock with preservative paste, oil and wax.
His cartridge pouch and shoes required frequent attention with
wax, to keep them waterproof. Much time had to be spent,
fastening and unfastening the many gaiter buttons with the gaiter
hook. The hair had to be smeared with wax, fastened tightly back
with ribbon, and then liberally sprinkled with powder. The locks
of hair at the side were curled up by a comrade or by the company

hairdresser. The grenadiers had the additional task of keeping their moustaches stiff and smooth with black wax and, in order to keep the points neat, they were sometimes tied up with thread before their owners went to bed.

During the same time the infantry of the Austrian Army also had to endure similar tribulations with clothing and equipment and they had the additional stricture of the stock - a neckcloth of stiff fabric, devised, so it is said, to force the soldiers' heads into an acceptable upright position. They also had to preen their hair in a similar style to their Prussian opponents.

In 1747 an order stipulated that their shoes were to show no creases (as this caused blistered feet on the march) and were to be neatly laced up. Shoes were to be changed around daily, as there were no 'lefts' and 'rights' in those days. A few years later a medical text book urged that shoes issued to the troops should be made of thick and strong leather, stitched with wax thread and smeared with wax so that water would not penetrate. Half boots (stretching above the ankle) were worn by the Hungarians, and by the Austrian infantry generally, from the late 1760s.

The fetish of spit and polish was well and truly launched by then and it reached a situation in the Austrian Army that the constant polishing of the musket barrels had caused them to become so thin that after a few live rounds had been fired, they were liable to burst, with unfortunate consequences to their owners.

Now and again a brake had to be applied to the system of loading men with more and more equipment and, in 1744, after experiments had been carried out at Potsdam by Frederick the Great, it was decreed that if time allowed the men would take off their knapsacks and all other equipment not immediately required before any action.

The evil invention of the stock made its way eventually to Britain and, after experiments had been made with linen stocks, the leather version was issued to the rank and file in 1786. The softer cloth type was at first taken into use to support the high collar of the regimental coat but when it was noted that as a result of the constriction of the throat and the chafing of the chin the soldier was forced to hold his head back and erect in, to some officers, a most pleasing military-looking fashion, the leather stock was brought in to ensure that the men continued to hold their heads erect. When the weather became hot or the soldier over-exerted himself in drill exercises or on a route march, however, cases of apoplexy were sometimes reported, resulting from tightly fitting stocks. Later, should their commanders permit it, on active service, men often unbuttoned their collars and turned their stocks outwards, away from the neck, so that they could breathe properly.

In addition to the discomfort of wearing the stock, the British soldier, through the Peninsular War and afterwards, was not only forced to wear equipment with straps which constricted the breathing, but had to carry loads which would have been well nigh unendurable on level ground, let alone the sometimes mountainous terrain and the vagaries of the Spanish weather which ranged from snow and ice to fierce summer heat. One unwilling authority on this subject was Rifleman John Harris of the 95th Rifles who recalled that:

> Many of our infantry sank and died under the weight of their knapsacks alone....So awkwardly was the load that our men bore, placed upon their backs, that the free motion of the body was impeded, the head held down from the pile at the back of the neck, and the soldier half beaten before he came to the scratch....Many a man died, I am convinced, who would have borne up well to the end of the retreat [to Corunna] but for the infernal load we carried on our backs.
>
> Being a tradesman, I marched under a weight sufficient to impede the free motions of a donkey; for besides my well-filled kit, there was the greatcoat rolled on its top, my blanket and camp kettle, my haversack, stuffed full of leather for repairing the men's shoes, together with a hammer and other tools, ship-biscuit and beef for three days. I also

carried my canteen filled with water, my hatchet and rifle and 80 rounds of ball cartridge in my pouch....

Altogether, the quantity of things I had on my shoulders was enough and more than enough for my needs, sufficient, indeed, to sink a little fellow of 5 feet 7 inches into the earth.

Other participants in the same campaign have recorded the items carried by men of the infantry regiments on the march. A typical load would consist of:

Musket and bayonet	14lbs in weight
Pouch & 60 rounds, ball cartridge	6lbs
Canteen and strap	1lb
Mess tin	1lb
Knapsack, frame & straps	3lbs
Blanket	4lbs
Greatcoat	4lbs
Dress coat	3lbs
White jacket	½lb
2 shirts & 3 breast-frills	2½lbs
2 pairs of boots	3lbs
1 pair of trousers	2lbs
1 pair of gaiters	¼lb
2 pairs of stockings	1lb
4 brushes, buttonstick & comb	3lbs
2 crossbelts	1lb
Pen, ink and paper	¼lb
Pipeclay, chalk etc	1lb
2 tent pegs	½lb
Bread	3lbs
Meat	2lbs
Water	3lbs
Total	59lbs (26.76kgs)

Some regiments operated a system whereby an iron camp kettle or a bill-hook were issues for every six men. Each mess of six drew lots to decide who should be cook the first day and carry the kettle and so on. The carrier of the bill-hook was decided by the same means.

It is reported that when the Duke of Wellington was asked what he thought was the first requirement of a good soldier, he replied 'a pair of boots, the second a pair of boots for a change, the third a pair of soles for repairs.' He learned this as a result of the Peninsular campaign when many men's shoes wore out when marching across country or because the footwear had been poorly made. In Craufurd's famous retreat to Corunna many officers and men marched with bare feet.

Sir Marc Isambard Brunel (father of Isambard Kingdom Brunel, who developed the steamships *Great Western*, *Great Eastern* and *Great Britain* and other works), himself an inventor of note, in his early years, in 1809 visited the naval dockyard at Portsmouth. He saw wounded soldiers from the Peninsular campaign being landed. Many of them were unshod and dragged themselves along the quays on lacerated, festering and rag-bandaged feet. They complained of shoes which broke up on the first day's march. Brunel obtained a few shoes of the type issued to the army and cut them up. Their defects were revealed - between the thin outer and inner soles was a filling of clay. When first issued the shoes appeared to be stoutly made and heavy but in the first puddle encountered on the march the clay dissolved like sugar candy. Brunel, already the inventor of a machine for mass-producing ships' pulley blocks, perceived that similar methods could be used for turning out military shoes. He set up a factory and recruited a number of disabled soldiers to operate a series of machines which produced good strong shoes in nine sizes. A variety of styles was manufactured on the machine - common and 'superior' shoes, water-boots, half-boots and 'Wellington' boots. Some of the Guards who fought at Waterloo a few years later wore footwear turned out on Brunel's machines.

Shoes were replaced in 1823 by ankle boots. The boots were issued without eyelet holes, the intention being that they should be pierced to suit the size of the wearer's feet. No distinction was made between right and left feet and in many regiments it was laid down that boots should be worn on alternate feet on alternate days in order to prevent uneven wear and to make the boots last longer (on the same principle that modern motorists should change their tyres periodically from wheel to wheel). The French Army issued their soldiers with three single boots, for easier rotation between the feet. In 1843 boots were issued in 'lefts' and 'rights' for the first time in the British Army, with eyelet holes provided for the laces.

For many years the old French soldier had been in the habit of wearing no socks and smeared his feet with tallow or fat. The great Marshal Saxe had been one of the first to see the advantages of such a practice. He said that by observing this precaution 'the feet never got excoriated on the march; dampness did not penetrate to them so easily, because it could not combat the grease.' Socks, on the other hand, besides being liable to shrink and so cause blistered feet, retained humidity and this led to conditions resulting in foot infections and soreness.

With a few variations, the equipment of the British soldier remained virtually unchanged from 1790 until the 1850s so that in the Crimean War the troops carried equipment similar in weight to that carried by their predecessors at Waterloo.

The British troops landing in the Crimea in 1854 wore a full dress uniform and carried a wooden canteen of water slung over one shoulder and over the other hung a haversack containing three days' rations. Each man carried a part of the mess cooking kit, a musket and a bayonet, a cartridge box and 50 rounds of ball ammunition. Instead of the usual pack or knapsack each soldier had to pack his small kit - towel, soap, razor, spare boots, two spare stocks, two shirts, two pairs of socks, boot blacking and brushes and a forage cap - into a roll or pack made out of a blanket, with a greatcoat or messtin on top. No matter how neatly and firmly the soldier rolled his blanket and affixed his greatcoat and messtin, it worked its way from the shoulders to the small of his back, causing great discomfort. In addition to this weight his full marching order consisted of two crossbelts, one holding the ammunition and pouch and the other the bayonet, fastened on the chest with a heavy regimental crossbelt plate. When fighting in the

Crimea the troops noted that the infantry of their French allies carried even more equipment and loads than they did.

A soldier in the 9th Regiment of Foot, serving in India during the Mutiny of 1857-58 wrote that a common soldier would fall in on parade, fully equipped, with 60 rounds of ammunition, a rifle and bayonet (weighing together 11½lbs), his haversack with two days' rations, and a water-bottle slung by his side and march away with his battalion. After travelling over eleven miles, nearly knee-deep in thick dust, the battalion would halt, the men almost dying for a drop of water. A soldier would be put on picquet duty all night. In the morning he was allowed to take his equipment off while he threw water over his hands and face to freshen himself up and, before he had time to drink a cup of coffee, the column was on the move again. Three or four days went by in this fashion, with no let-up, in all kinds of weather and at all hours of the day and night. Half the time the men were not even told where they were going or what was happening.

Similar experiences befell troops labouring under the milder sun of Europe. One Prussian soldier recalled how he opened the front of his shirt on the march and 'the steam rose as if from a boiling kettle.'

A more relaxed attitude prevailed among some soldiers in the Army of Northern Virginia in the American Civil War of 1861-65. They found that boots were not agreeable on a long march. They were 'heavy and irksome' and when the heels became a little one-sided through wear, the wearer would find his ankle twisted nearly out of joint by the unevenness of the road. When the boots became wet they were hard to remove and even worse when they had to be pulled on at morning roll-call. Some men obtained strong brogue shoes or brogans, with broad bottoms and big flat heels and wore these instead of the boots and found them comfortable to wear and easier to pull on and off. The average soldier kept his belongings to the minimum to avoid the extra weight and wore a jacket, hat, shirt, one pair of pants, one pair of drawers, one pair of shoes and a pair of socks. His baggage consisted of one blanket, one rubber blanket (presumably used as a ground sheet) and one haversack. This latter generally contained tobacco and a pipe, soap and additional rations of apples, black-berries and other commodities gathered on the line of march.

Company cooking kit consisted of two or three skillets and frying pans, which were sometimes carried on the waggons but more often carried by the infantryman. (It was not unknown for a soldier to stick the handle of a frying pan in the barrel of a musket and so carry it - a practice which, doubtless, would have produced a choleric reaction from any sergeant-major of an infantry regiment in any European armies of the period.) Confeder-ate troops gradually discarded their peaked 'soldier hats' and replaced them with more comfortable soft and floppy slouch hats, and likewise discarded knapsacks and heavy cap and cartridge boxes, preferring to carry their contents in their coat pockets. Tin cups were preferred to the army issue canteens and gloves were thrown away after being found useless when the men handled their axes, loaded muskets and used ramrods. Some men thought that bayonets were not of much use so did not hesitate to cast them aside with their scabbards.

It was about this time that the Prussian Army introduced the marching boot later to be generally (if incorrectly) known as the jackboot.[2] This first pattern was shorter for a time and was then raised to just over mid-calf height. More experiments were carried out with types of loads to be carried by front-line infantry and, as a result, just before the outbreak of the Franco-Prussian War in 1870, a light battle order was devised, based on a rolled greatcoat, with messtins and spare ammunition.

In 1902 a high-ranking officer of the French Army wrote an authoritative work about the weight of kit carried by infantry of the major armies of Europe and the United States. He revealed that the 28.5 kilograms weight carried by American infantry was the heaviest of any army, but the largest load of any *unit* was the 32 kilos pack, etcetera of the French Chasseurs Alpins. German soldiers carried 26.7 kilos, Russian 26.4, French 24.4 (plus a section

---

[2] In military parlance the first jackboots were riding boots which reached over the knee - the British Life Guards and the Blues and Royals mounted troops wear a version of these.

of tent that weighed an additional 2.6 kilos). British soldiers carried 23.6 kilos, with a mean weight of 26.5 kilos (about 58lbs).

One former member of the French Foreign Legion in 1911 wrote that the men did not wear socks inside their boots. Some wore pieces of linen, called *chausettes Russes* or Russian socks, wrapped round their feet but the majority of legionnaires preferred to wear nothing between their bare feet and the leather. This practice did not seem to affect the marching ability of the Legion and distances of 25 miles a day in the blistering desert were known, whilst carrying 100lbs of equipment.

The infantry of the First World War carried colossal loads on their backs. The French *poilu*'s burden weighed 85lbs. The weight of the pack has been described as 'monumental and crushing.' It contained not only the regulation items but also the man's little treasures and comforts - tins of fruit, chocolate, candles and so on.

The penalties of carrying too-heavy loads were tragically illustrated on July 1st 1916, the first day of the Battle of the Somme. After a heavy bombardment of the German trenches British infantry attacked. They had previously marched from the villages and forming-up points behind the line and had stumbled their way through winding communication trenches which stretched for a mile or so from the front line proper. On their way they gathered a growing mound of stores, including 200 rounds of ammunition each, in cloth bandoliers and boxes, new empty sandbags (to fortify the positions they hoped to capture), a wiring stake for the same purpose, grenades and shovels and some were given rockets and pigeon baskets to carry. Each man was already wearing a full issue of heavy webbing equipment and personal belongings, including a blanket and greatcoat, as well as a rifle or Lewis gun, bayonet and entrenching tool. The whole load must have been at least 60lbs. When the additional items they had collected up to the line were included the total weight must have been in the region of 100lbs. Not only that, but some individuals had to help carry heavy cumbersome rolls of barbed wire.

When the time of attack was signalled they had to climb the storming ladders, scramble over the trench parapet and work their way forward. Some carried their rifles sloped or at the port position, others were bent forward like men fighting their way through heavy winds and rain, with bayonets fixed and the rifles held at the 'On Guard' position.

Under heavy machine-gun fire and explosions from the enemy mortar and artillery positions those more fortunate reached the German wire entanglements, uncut from their own preliminary artillery barrage, and fell, trying to find a way through. Thousands perished that day. Because of the weight of their equipment and the load they carried, men could only walk slowly forward over the torn-up earth and shell-holes, thus presenting a perfect target to the enemy.

In the endless arguments and masses of literature discussing the failure of that first day of the Battle of the Somme most now agree that a major factor which contributed to the tragic failure was the enormous loads heaped on to the attacking infantry. 'They made it difficult to get out of a trench, impossible to move more quickly than a slow walk or to rise and lie down quickly.'

The basic equipment of the British soldier in the First World War had been designed to distribute the load he was expected to carry equally around his body. It had first been issued in 1908 and consisted of a wide waistbelt of webbing to which were attached cartridge pouches, shoulder straps, haversack, a large pack or valise worn on the back, all made of the same material, plus water-bottle, entrenching tool, and bayonet in a leather scabbard in a webbing frog. It was the *extra* weight which the men had been ordered to carry in 1916 that contributed to the disaster.

The khaki service dress, worn with long puttees, served the British soldier all through the war and, in the Guards regiments, into the Second World War for a short time.

After the 1914-18 war the German Army experimented for a time with laced and buckled high boots but reverted to the old and popular *Marschstiefel* (jack-boot), affectionately known as *Knobelbecher* (dice-box) until the last years of the Second World War when a shortage of leather caused them to be replaced by an ankle boot, worn with short canvas gaiters.

Preliminary sketch for painting showing the 6th Air-landing Brigade advancing across fields towards Hamminkeln after the gliderborne assault over the Rhine in March 1945

By the start of the 1939-45 war British soldiers wore a khaki battledress, consisting of a short blouse jacket, and trousers designed to be buttoned at the ankle. Eventually, short puttees were worn, then anklets made of webbing. The webbing equipment, first issued in 1937, was lighter and easier to wear and adjust than the 1908 pattern.

The faithful British ammunition ankle boot was of a sturdy pattern and when first issued to recruits was in its natural leather colour. After treatment with a raw potato, much application of black boot polish and treated to hours of spit-and-polishing in small circles, it was possible to obtain a mirror-like gloss to the leather. In regimental depots recruits experimented with the bowls of spoons heated on top of a stove to iron out the pimples in the leather and a more extreme (and officially forbidden) trick was to heap thick applications of boot polish on to the toes and uppers of the boots and set fire to it. After the flames had been blown out quickly, more polish was applied and the spit-and-polish process repeated. The polish-burning system had the effect of damaging the stitching in the welt and upper and lower soles and other parts of the boot, with uncomfortable results for the wearer in later route marches and field exercises in wet weather.

The German jack-boot made its re-appearance in 1953 in the West German Border Guard and in 1957 to the Bundeswehr. The fitting of the boot was the secret of comfortable wear. In one quoted instance the soldier's company, platoon and section commanders, assisted by the company sergeant major and the company quartermaster sergeant checked the recruit's first issue of jack-boots. He had to waterproof them and soften the uppers. For long route marches the soldier could secure his heels in the boot, to prevent them rubbing and causing blisters, by wearing *Marschriemen*, simply the straps and tabs of spurs minus the spur itself and jokingly referred to as *Infanteriesporen* (infantryman's spurs). It has always been considered by the German soldier that to pull off a jack-boot is simpler than undoing boot laces or buckles. To cross a deep water obstacle the boots could be pulled off and a bare-footed crossing made. In the case of a proper assault, at a convenient moment the boots could be pulled off and emptied quicker than a soldier wearing ordinary laced boots.

In recent years the Bundeswehr (West German Army) has found that modern recruits' feet 'are too tender for the jack-boot.' After many complaints had been made by young soldiers, some were sent by their medical officers to an orthopaedic specialist who issued prescriptions for lace-up high jumping boots instead of the jack-boot. Jack-boots are still worn by the Soviet Army, the East German People's Army and some of the armies of the Warsaw Pact.

The army of the United States experimented with a number of types of marching boot during the Second World War. The soldiers first wore ankle boots and high canvas leggings then graduated to a stout ankle boot with sewn-on leather gaiters, buckled at the sides. The parachutists wore an excellent high lace-up boot, brown in colour, which were much sought after by the men of the Allied armies. Galoshes were issued to men in the European theatre of war and many disparaging remarks were passed by observers watching long files of American troops 'padding along' the sides of roads, wearing galoshes, only about half being secured by their snap-fastenings so that the two loose 'wings' flapped about like those on the feet of the Roman god Mercury.

The Pentagon once again sent their men out to war overladen with kit. The American doughboy landing in North Africa for Operation Torch shouldered nearly 132lbs per man while the marines in the Pacific, carrying a basic load of 84.3lbs, waded through the surf on Japanese-held islands, sometimes struggling with extra loads of 20lb automatic rifles, 45lb mortar base-plates or 47lb mortar bipods.

The American authorities still failed to learn anything in the 1960s when the army was sent to fight in Vietnam. One man went into battle with 350 M16 rounds, six fragmentation grenades, one phosphorous and two smoke grenades, 2,000 rounds in a machine-gun belt, three days' rations and two full canteens. Some soldiers' packs were so heavy that they disinclined to crawl when under fire because they were so tired it was easier to move by keeping to their feet.

One aspect of equipment which was particularly severely tested by British troops in the Falklands campaign of 1982 was personal clothing. Since the 1960s the soldier wore the familiar and well-tested ammunition boot, with leather soles, hobnails and heel plates but the direct-moulded sole (DMS) boot with rubber sole was considered to be more flexible to march in, so it was brought into service. This type of boot was, like its predecessor, water-resistant but not waterproof. Leather has to 'breathe' and making it completely waterproof creates more problems than it would solve since the sweat trapped inside would rapidly cause all sorts of foot problems. The main problem of the ankle-boot is that water seeps through the lace-holes and in the boggy conditions of the Falklands this led to an epidemic of trench foot, resulting in about forty men having to be evacuated for treatment. The fact that puttees were also worn was an added inconvenience in the time taken to unwinding them and taking the boots off for the feet to be dried and dry socks put on. The quality of the high lace-up boots of the Argentinians was noted and some of the British units gave their men much latitude in their choice of a similar kind of footwear.

A new Boot, Combat, High (BCH) has been issued and, apart from reaching above the ankle, the tongue is sealed to the inside of the boot, which should prevent water from seeping through the lace-holes. This boot is to be combined with a Moisture Vapour Permeable (MVP) inner sock, a new technology product which allows sweat to be evaporated through it but keeps water out.

This type of high lace-up boot is fairly standard in armies world-wide and for ease of putting on and taking off is an improvement on the old combination of boots and puttees or gaiters. It was considered that they provided excellent ankle support and the only drawback is that they are not suitable for running on tarmac or concrete roads or across rough country over long distances. However, the authorities considering the question came to the conclusion that with the increasing use of personnel carriers the troops would not be required to march long distances and, in any event, stout training shoes could be worn when completing fitness training exercises.

(A recent report about the British high combat boot suggests that because of the constriction occasioned above the ankle, cases of Achilles tendon trouble have been increasing. Training shoes are allowed to be worn already on fitness training exercises because of the unsuitability of the BCH pattern footwear. It would appear that the boot now issued might not be the correct answer for negotiating rough country and a lower pattern might re-appear in due course.)

The Falklands campaign revealed that men could not be taken to the battlefield on every occasion in personnel carriers because the nature of the ground precluded their use. It also rekindled the old argument whether men could carry out their duties whilst carrying heavy loads. Critics remembered that this was an important factor which contributed to the slaughter on the Somme in 1916 and questioned why men in the 1980s were still being called upon to advance across difficult country whilst heavily laden. A commander states that while certain units of 3 Commando Brigade advanced across East Falkland carrying heavy equipment in record time, they had to do so at a speed not much quicker than a slow walk.

Another commander, of 45 Marine Commando, carried over 83lbs of equipment in the attack on Two Sisters Hill. This included not only his rifle, bayonet, night sight, five full magazines, three grenades and a bandolier of 50 rounds, but also a 24-hour ration pack, water and radio. He stated that all his kit was necessary and anyone sending his men into a battle of that nature with less equipment would be 'pushing his luck.' It was not possible for any soldier to strip his kit of non-essentials (in his estimation) and go into action, and then go back in the dark and pick up the other items he might need, while being shelled and anticipating an immediate counter-attack on the position that had just been captured.

The modern soldier is usually fortunate that more often than not his pack or Bergen will be flown to him in his new position by helicopter, brought up before nightfall in his company's transport or will simply stay in his unit's armoured personnel carrier. In today's modern armies, with their emphasis on lightning infantry advances across country in personnel carriers, instead of long columns of infantry winding along dusty or muddy roads, an officer of the Soviet Army can still find an argument for his troops wearing calf-length leather boots in action. He reasons that, besides their historical and traditional significance, the boots keep the soldiers' feet healthy and are warmer and drier than the ankle or 'high combat' boot in severe weather conditions, after jumping from their APCs, sometimes into puddles and other muddy conditions. They can also be removed more quickly in the case of injury or wounds. Instead of socks the Soviet soldier of today still wears strips of linen (of summer or winter thickness) wound round his feet when wearing calf-length boots.

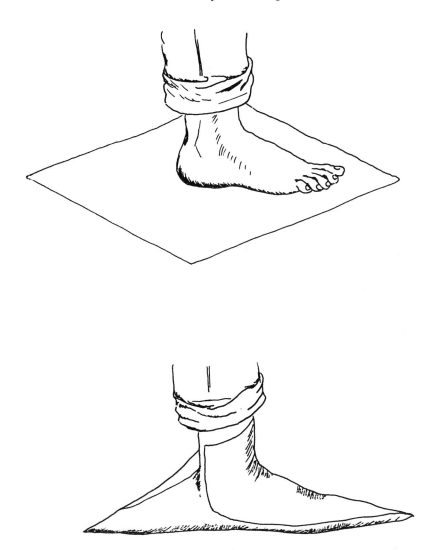

Sketch showing the method of wrapping foot in a cloth before pulling on infantry calf-length boot - a method still used in the Soviet and DDR People's Armies

A fact that will interest sergeant majors of the British Army is that when the Soviet Army withdrew from Afghanistan a year or so ago, on orders from the Kremlin the 80,000 conscripts of the raggle-taggle Afghan Army were issued with tins of boot polish. The idea behind the issue was that the gleaming boots, it was hoped, would improve the apparently low morale of the troops left behind to resist the anti-communist tribesmen attacking the centre of population.

The subject of boot polish is one which is made known to an army recruit from his first days in the regimental depot. In the nineteenth century the cleaning of military footwear was a laborious business of applying wax, lamp-black or other substance to the leather. Cases have been known where unusual substances such as soap, glue, gum arabic, molasses, white-of-egg, molasses and beer were used to develop a satisfactory gleam to the boot or shoe.

In 1906 a new polish, given the name of Kiwi, was invented in Melbourne, Australia. It contained ingredients which nourished the leather and kept it supple. It was water resistant and unaffected by the vagaries of the climate. With the outbreak of the First World War there came an enormous demand for the polish. Millions of men under arms meant that there were millions of boots to be polished, as well as leather leggings, bandoliers, and equipment for horses and men. Between the wars the distribution became worldwide and included countries later to be at war with one another in 1939. A correspondent wrote from Tobruk in 1942 that 'old tins of British-made Kiwi polish lay side by side with empty bottles of Chianti,' from the former Italian garrison.

Within the last few years the same company has succeeded in bringing out a new kind of polish. Called 'Parade Gloss' it is made of Carnauba wax, a hard vegetable wax from Brazil (for the shine); a mineral wax extracted from brown coal (to improve the gloss) and paraffin wax (for its preservative effects). This polish could prove to be the recruits' dream substance - it requires no spit-and-polish techniques. The polish is rubbed in with a damp cloth until a shine appears. A perfect gloss is then obtained by finishing off with a soft brush.

So, despite the passage of centuries, the twinkling toecap is still one of the transcending virtues of the foot soldier, apparently.

Chapter Seven

Arduous Marches

It has been said that an individual in fair health and vigour, walking unencumbered, can travel along a good road at the rate of 3½ to 4 miles an hour with ease; but the same man, if loaded with arms, kit, ammunition and provisions, will not be able to maintain that pace for long. Let him march in a column of route with others, taking care not to collide with those on each side of him nor those in front, and his pace will certainly slacken. Again, let him form part of a body of troops, exposed to frequent stops and starts, distressed by heat and dust, tortured by fatigue and thirst and he can just about move forward.

The ultimate stages of tiredness and misery is often endured by the soldier - soaked in rain or sweat, soiled by mud or covered with sticky dust, exhausted, probably deprived of water and rations, reeling under the weight of weapons and equipment, yet urged on by his NCOs, comrades or his own will-power.

Arguments about the length of a particular march, the time taken to complete it and the approximate weight carried are, in the main, pointless as there will always be disagreements about superlatives such as 'the longest', 'the fastest', 'the most difficult' and so on. What can be done, therefore, is to set out the circum-stances of marches from the pages of history and let the reader, from his knowledge and experience, try to appreciate the physical and mental strain imposed on those taking part in a particular exploit.

When pupils are taught at school that King Harold 'hurried to meet William in Sussex in 1066 after defeating Tostig and Harold Hardrada at the battle of Stamford Bridge in Yorkshire' they do not always appreciate, nor is it explained to them by their teachers, the sheer effort required by those who had to march the whole distance of 250 miles, on poor paths and cross country, carrying spears, javelins, heavy swords or cumbersome Danish-style battle-axes, shields and, for the more better off, helmets and coats of mail, as well as provisions to sustain them on their march southwards.

In comparing the marches of Cromwell's infantry and those of later periods it is always necessary to take into account the load each soldier had to carry. In ordinary marching order the British infantry now carries a load of about 40lbs and, during the Peninsular War, according to Wellington, they carried about 60lbs. The foot soldier of the seventeenth century and, more specifically, those who fought in the latter part of the English Civil War, carried heavier loads then either.

The pike and matchlock were weighty and, being awkward to carry, seemed even heavier to the men equipped with them. The ammunition of a musketeer, taking into account the powder flask, match, bandoliers and the pouch with its weight of bullets, must have seemed almost a penance to him. The metal helmet and corselet of the pikeman were an intolerable burden on a long march and the abandonment of his defensive armour later in the war was due to this fact. Finally, both pikemen and musketeers had their knapsacks in which they frequently carried as much as seven days' provisions and, during the campaigns in Ireland and Scotland, they sometimes carried a portion of a tent.

Bearing these facts in mind, one of their commanders, describing a raid made by his troops into the quarters of the Irish rebels, paid this tribute:

> For my Foot, I think they are as good as ever marched, either for fighting, searching woods or bogs, or for long and speedy marching. I dare say they marched, last Wednesday and Thursday, before they rested, at least thirty miles, and much of it through woods and bogs, almost never on a road, continuing marching night and day. All this march, I never heard any of them complain he was weary or lame; it was hard to keep them from straggling before, but very easy to keep them up in the rear. Our horsemen did all confess, their horses were not

able to continue a march with them; almost one half of our Horse being lame and tired, though they had every night good lodging, and as good provision of oats and hay as they could desire. My Foot were many times beating the woods and bogs, when the horse stood still and looked on.[1]

Nearly every schoolchild in Britain has heard of the famous victory at Blenheim in 1704 but few know the details of the historic march of Marlborough's troops which preceded it. Even today, the details of the 'March to the Danube' are taught to young recruits of the West German Bundeswehr, as an example of the dogged marching ability of British infantry and the sound military logistics that were involved.

The operation involved moving a force of 40,000 horse, foot and artillery 250 miles from the Netherlands to the banks of the Danube. The troops were constantly on the march for six weeks and arrived at their destination fit for battle, with not a man lost through sickness and privation. Meticulous organisation ensured adequate supplies of bread, meat and forage at each night's halt, as a result of arrangements made in advance, even ordering 12,000 pairs of new shoes in readiness for the halfway stage. March discipline was such that the local populace on the route had not a single complaint to make about the soldiers' conduct.

In diaries kept by men involved it was said that by beginning each day's march by sunrise, before it became unbearably hot, the troops were settling in their new camps by early afternoon. As the Commissaries had brought to the ground all the necessaries for horse and foot before the columns arrived, the soldiers had little to do except pitch their tents, boil their kettles and settle down to rest.

---

[1] This situation was repeated nearly three hundred years later when the infantry of the 6th Airborne Division, during the 1945 drive to the Baltic, had to work their way forward to search woods and copses to ensure that they were clear of German armour and self-propelled anti-tank guns so that their own 'cavalry' (tanks), lying hull-down behind them, could resume their advance.

It is recorded that Marlborough himself, seeing some of his infantry drop to the ground, suffering from exhaustion, instructed that some of them should be carried in his own coach. The daily distance covered averaged 12 to 14 miles a day, a comparatively comfortable span for men and draught animals alike.

Anyone considering the march should, once again, take into account the way the men were clothed and equipped. Although it was, generally, a hot summer, the uniform worn by the foot soldier consisted of a long and rather loose-fitting coat, with the skirts usually looped back to facilitate marching. A waistcoat was worn and the usual headgear was of black felt or beaver, three-cornered and looped up at the sides. Men of the grenadier companies wore tall mitre-shaped caps which allowed the soldier to more easily sling his musket before he threw a grenade.

When the weather sometimes broke, torrential rain rendered the roads near impassable as the infantry struggled through the thick mud churned up by the artillery and cavalry. When the columns reached the banks of the Danube, picked detachments fought their way up a hill and drove the French and Bavarians off the crest, under heavy fire. After a period of rest the army marched rapidly from its quarters and, after hours of complicated manoeuvres over rough ground, shattered the Franco-Bavarian Army at Blenheim on August 2nd 1704.

During the War of Spanish Succession (1702-1713) the campaigns of Marlborough were marked by the number of arduous night marches before his main battles and engagements. In nearly every case it was found that the infantry had to wade nearly knee-deep in clay and dirt because the cavalry ahead had broken up the already poor roads. It was reported that the greater part of one battalion of the Welch Fusiliers marched without shoes -some had been sucked off the men's feet by the mud and others had disintegrated because of hard wear. One dispatch mentioned that the troops left camp at three o'clock one afternoon and marched all night. They continued marching until three o'clock in the afternoon of that day, experiencing appalling conditions because of the broken-up, muddy roads and covered only twelve miles in the whole 24 hours.

Marlborough's men were said to have marched easily, almost casually, at a slow pace, in the most difficult of country, along muddy roads and across ploughed fields. They did not move in strict step to a drumbeat when the enemy was not near to threaten danger. At Mainz the 1st Battalion of the First Guards were congratulated on their handsome appearance, and the cleanliness of their arms, accoutrements, clothes, shoes and linen were also favourably reported upon. The infantry sang 'Lilliburlero' and 'Over the Hills and Far Away' as they marched along.

The British were not the only troops to have made a memorable march to the Danube. In 1805 the French Army marched from the shores of the English Channel (where they had been encamped, preparing to invade England, before plans were changed) to the banks of the Rhine - a mean distance of 400 miles. The troops covered the distance in 27 days, marching an average 14.8 miles a day. There were many conscripts in the ranks but they endured manfully. After a series of marches and manoeuvres the Austrian Army was defeated. The French Army, with Napoleon at its head, crossed the valley of the Danube and entered Vienna. Soon afterwards the decisive battle of Austerlitz was fought in which the Austrian and Russian Armies were crushed.

A dispatch from the Peninsula in January 1809 includes the bare details of the distances between towns on the route of the British Army during its retreat to Corunna. It was estimated that the rearguard would have had to march 135 miles in about nine days. A recent estimate reckons that some of the British infantry, in the course of the entire Peninsular campaign, fought and marched over 6,000 miles. These figures, although formidable, give no picture of the actual sufferings of some of the participants. When one is able to read the actual words of a soldier who took part, however, the sheer heroism of some of the infantry is beyond belief.

On the retreat to Corunna a soldier of the 71st (Highland) Regiment of Foot, whose name, alas, is not known, described the dreadful nature of the forced march from Astorga. The first sixteen miles of the road led straight up a mountain, a barren waste of snow. All the way up he heard the groans of the men who, unable to march any further, had laid down to perish at the side of the road. He himself marched in a state of torpor. The rain poured down in torrents, the melted snow was half knee-deep in places and stained by the blood flowing from wounded and bruised feet. In turns they were forced to drag along the heavy baggage trains. On New Year's Day 1809 they were drenched with rain, famished with cold and hunger and fearful of what might happen to them if they were picked up by the pursuing French. Time and time again they had to turn and fight off the enemy. With the few remaining waggons carrying their women and children they turned and resumed their retreat. From the dead they obtained scraps of food and serviceable shoes but many survivors had to walk barefooted as their footwear had worn out. Even some officers were forced to wrap their feet in pieces of old blankets. They eventually reached Corunna and, after a few days wait and fierce fighting with the French, they completed their embarkation.

The most rapid recorded march by foot soldiers is said to be one of 62 miles in 26 hours on 28th-29th July 1809 by the British Light Brigade under Brigadier-General (later Major-General) Robert Craufurd, coming to the relief of Lieutenant-General Sir Arthur Wellesley, later Field Marshal the 1st Duke of Wellington, after the battle of Talavera in the Peninsular War.

One of the most appalling marches ever recorded was that of Napoleon's Grand Army's retreat from Moscow in 1812. A captain in that army kept a diary and remembered how he wore a boot and an old shoe on his feet, carried a crutch to help him walk and was dressed in a pink cloak lined with ermine, and a hood over his head. He and his companions ate from the horses which died every day and, as he was in the rearguard, he did not get the best of cuts from the unfortunate animals. Horseflesh was eaten half-cooked and he was sprinkled with grease and blood from his chin to his knees. His face was filthy and he had a long beard. There were long icicles on their hair and beards. Those who had neither knife, sabre nor axe and whose hands were frozen, could not eat. He had seen soldiers on their knees, and others, sitting near the carcasses of horses and biting at the flesh like hungry wolves. For drink they had snow, melted in a saucepan.

The situation of the wounded, sick and those with amputated limbs, was awful and they lay, huddled in carts, of which the horses had died of fatigue and hunger. These poor wretches were left abandoned at the bivouacs and on the road and many died insane. Those who had the strength killed themselves. The companions and friends of these poor creatures, who could offer no help, turned away their eyes so as not to see them.

The sun never appeared and the strong wind covered them with snow, which froze on them. Soon it was difficult to see the road, except for the mounds which covered the corpses of men and animals. Some had died with their hands in the air, and were frozen in that position. Those with frozen hands could not hold their weapons and as they wandered about were driven away by those fortunate enough to have bivouac fires, because they could not contribute any food to the stock. As they died, outside of those circled round the fire, others stripped them of their clothes and possessions.

Soldiers affected by the extreme cold sometimes fell down and their fingers and thumbs snapped like glass. One captain of infantry took off the bandages in which his feet had been wrapped and three toes came off with it. He removed the rags from his other foot and, taking hold of the big toe, twisted it round and pulled it off, without feeling any pain. He went through the rest of the retreat thus mutilated and died in Italy from the result of his wounds.

Soon, the different parts of the army almost ceased to exist and their fragments were formed into small societies of six, eight or ten men, who marched together, had their stock of food in common and drove away any person who did not belong to their gang. All these men huddled together on the march, like sheep and taking care not to be separated from his gang, and being ill-treated by those in other groups, who would take his food and drive him away from them.

60,000 men were left, each carrying a sack, supporting himself with a stick, clothed in dirty rags and eaten up with vermin. Faces were hideous, yellow and smoked, smeared with earth, blackened by the greasy smoke of pine fires, the eyes hollow, the beard covered with snot and ice. Hands could not be used to button up the trousers and many fastened them up with a piece of cord. They were all indescribably filthy and several days went by without washing or still less, to change their clothes. Such was the spectacle of an army which, eight months before, had been the finest in the world.

When the survivors reached a town or village, the fittest crowded into the houses for shelter and drove the others away who sometimes set fire to the dwellings, burning the inhabitants as well as the new lodgers. Sometimes, the houses, which were built of wood, were pulled down and taken to the bivouacs to make rough shelters. A fire would be lighted, flour and water kneaded together and these 'dampers' cooked on the ashes. Pieces of horseflesh would be taken from sacks and thrown on the embers to get cooked.

The diarist lived on this kind of fare for over three weeks, without salt or bread, though he occasionally managed to obtain barley, rye or oat cake. Dough was made of any sort of flour, mixed with snow water. It was a black mixture and full of sand. Some gunpowder from cartridges was mixed with it, for powder is salt, and, at all events, made the food less insipid to the taste. The meal being finished, everybody crowded round the fire and went to sleep, to get some strength to resist the morrow's sufferings. At daybreak, without drum or trumpet, the army resumed its march back to France.

In the days before troop trains were available the infantry, of course, were obliged to march everywhere and with the ever-expanding British Empire her troops were called upon to travel immense distances, even in peacetime when 'Change of Station' excursions were commonplace.

One extraordinary march has hardly received the notice it deserves. That it was a remarkable exploit is vouched for by the fact that on its being reported to the Duke of Wellington, he remarked that it was one of the greatest feats ever performed and he envied the achievement of the officer commanding. It involved the 43rd of Foot and a winter march across the Portage of the Madawaska in Canada in December 1837.

The First Division of the regiment, consisting of 78 officers and men, left their barracks at Fredericton in a temperature of zero degrees Fahrenheit. At first 14 two-horse sleds were used to contain the men, provisions, ammunition and baggage and eight men were squeezed into some of the sleds, which were only supposed to hold six. The River St. John was crossed on the ice, thence on the bank, completing a journey of 39 miles. The First Division was followed by a company of the regiment each succeeding day, approximately equal in strength to the first contingent, until six companies in all were travelling the same route.

Travelling across rivers on the dangerous ice or being ferried across on flat-bottomed scows or canoes lashed together, in temperatures several degrees below zero took five days to travel 132 miles. Some of the rivers were from 150 to 200 yards wide, fast-flowing and some of the sled drivers and ferrymen had to stand up to their middles in the icy water, helped by some of the soldiers, tugging some of the grounded craft off the bottom of the rivers.

During the days following some of the men were frost-bitten and so numb that they had to get out of the sleds and run to restore their circulation. On one day the forest track became impassable to sleds and the troops were compelled to trudge through knee-deep snow for three days at a stretch. Snowstorms during the night on one occasion covered the sleds completely and the horses nearly buried.

Each company had been provided with a dozen pairs of snowshoes and, as there had not been time to practise the men in their use beforehand, they thought they could march better without them. One company, however, persisted in using them and found them very helpful. One particular difficulty experienced on the march was the steepness and constant succession of hills. At one time, the snow never being less than knee-deep at every step and in some places double that, the unit did not accomplish the day's distance until 7 o'clock at night. The men were overcome by fatigue. Their sleds did not arrive for nearly two hours afterwards, having taken 11½ hours to travel 15 miles.

The First Division reached its destination at Quebec, having accomplished a distance of 370 miles in 18 days and was followed by the rest of the regiment, with but one casualty -a private who had been left sick at Madawaska.

The history of India provides many examples of long or swift marches performed by Anglo-Indian forces. What told so severely on the British troops was the intense heat of the climate but despite this the troops were often called upon to march in the hottest season and sometimes during the searing heat of the middle part of the day.

In 1845 when the Sikhs invaded British territory several remarkable marches were carried out by the British troops and the Indians under their command. In the space of seven days British infantry marched 155 miles and fought the Sikhs at Moodkee on the last day. Their fatigue, the heat and the dust were beyond description. The country was dead flat and covered with thorny jungle; the roads were unmetalled - often mere tracks - and very heavy for marching, owing to the deep sand. The heat was oppressive during the day, clouds of dust smothered the soldiers, there was little water and often it was impossible to cook any food for, owing to the slow pace of the camels and the still slower pace of the bullock-carts, the cooking utensils did not come up until far too late. It was agreed that 'altogether it was a most harassing march.' It was also remarked that in the First Sikh War the Indian sepoys did not seem to have the same stamina and physical endurance as their British counterparts despite the fact that most of them should have been more used to the climate and conditions of the area.

One of the British infantry's more protracted change-of-station marches started at the town of Allahabad, India in 1853, when the 52nd Foot commenced their move to Umballa, some 500 miles distant. The day started at 3 am. when the first deep notes of the 'Rouse' were heard. The tents were then struck, rolled up and loaded on to elephants whilst the bedding was buckled to camels, all with the utmost difficulty. At last the men fell in and were then marched to the road, where the column was formed up.

Leaving the baggage in the charge of a guard detachment, the battalion was given the order to march.

The troops marched in silence at first and some, still half asleep, rolled a few paces out of the ranks, until checked by their comrades or NCOs. At the end of the first hour the regiment halted. At the side of the road some five or six large coppers, full of hot coffee, awaited the men. After a short halt, the bugle sounded, the men fell in and the band struck up a lively march as the column moved off. In a couple of hours the sun rose and, after some of the men finished smoking their pipes, one man would

Troops taking a coffee break in India during a long distance change-of-station march circa 1897

generally start a song and the rest joined in. The singing was not always possible unless there was a side wind, as the dust rose in clouds from the marching feet and hung over the column. It was worse in the rear than in the front so, in order that everybody should have a fair chance, the company marching in the rear on one day would lead the column the following day.

'Camp colour men' were sent ahead of the column and were responsible for marking out the new camp site. The baggage train was never far behind the marching troops and once they were halted it did not take long for the tents to be pitched and breakfasts served.

En route there was time for the officers to indulge in their favourite pursuits of game shooting until the time for bed for everybody - at 8 pm. Day after day the routine continued, although there was generally a halt on Sunday, when divine service was performed in the main street of the camp.

The usual marching season was in the winter when rains seldom fell. Every morning the regiment found itself in a strange place; and, although in the plains the scenery was not varied, every halting-place was different from the last. Occasionally, a place would be reached and a challenge made to the regiment stationed there, for a game of cricket. Occasionally, despite the vigilance of the picquets, men would wake up and find a hole had been cut in their tent during the night and all their possessions stolen. The headman of the 'bazaar', which followed the regiment and his trackers would try to follow the thieves across country by tracking their footmarks.

Arriving at Cawnpore the regiment was welcomed by the 70th Foot, which lined the road to welcome them in. The 52nd were horrified at their white and sickly appearance as they were just recovering from an epidemic of cholera. (The 52nd, two and a half years afterwards, looked just as bad, if not worse, after a similar outbreak of the disease). The regiment made its way, steadily, up the country, marching about ten miles each day and eventually arrived at Umballa, where it was to be stationed.

A splendid feat of marching was that of the 43rd Light Infantry during the Indian Mutiny. In 1858 the regiment, then at

Bangalore, received a route for Kamptee, a distance of 631 miles. All weekly men having been weeded out, the regiment set out and reached its destination, only to be ordered to proceed 156 miles to Jubbulpore, thence to Banda, where they joined General Whitelock's Division. After the capture of Kirwee the 43rd was divided into two sections and sent to different places, then brought together again and marched off to Calpee. When they arrived there the men had marched a total of 1,300 miles.

Some idea of the excessive exertion and fatigue undergone by the troops can be judged from the records which show that the march was in most part performed during the hottest season of the year in which the mean temperature exceeded in heat that of any known during the fifteen preceding seasons.

The marches commenced before daylight, usually as early as 2 am. and it frequently happened that the rear of the column did not arrive in camp until 4 or 5 pm. A mere country track constituted the only route, at times crossing chains of precipitous hills, cutting through rocks and jungles for days together, traversing and passing numerous rivers, many of great breadth, without bridges or boats. Now and again the regiment was employed in dragging carts - some hundreds in number - containing ammunition and stores over almost insurmountable obstacles, where cattle were nearly useless.

Under these trying circumstances the regiment kept its good health extraordinarily well but in the end the amount of wear and tear endured began to tell on the men's constitution. Sunstroke was of constant occurrence and death generally most sudden. From this and miscellaneous causes during the march 3 officers and 44 men died.

Several notable marches were carried out by infantry of both the Union and Confederate armies in the American Civil War which began in 1861. General 'Stonewall' Jackson's troops covered 51 miles in 24 hours in 1862 and the Union Army accomplished distances of 35 miles in one day in June and July of 1863. One soldier described vividly what exactly lies behind the prosaic statements of so many miles covered in such and such a time. He stated that troops on the march were generally so cheerful and gay that an outsider, looking at them as they marched by, would hardly imagine how they suffered. In summertime the dust, combined with the heat, caused much anguish. The nostrils, eyes and throat felt the effects and dust was collected in the hair and ears. The shoes became full of sand and the dust, penetrating the clothes and getting in at the neck, wrists and ankles and mixed with sweat, produced an irritant as active as cantharides. Their heavy woollen uniforms were a great annoyance and it was thought that linen or cotton clothing would have been much better. If the dust and heat were not present to annoy, so mud, cold, rain, snow, hail and wind took over. Rain was the greatest discomfort a soldier could suffer. Wet clothes, shoes and blankets; wet meat and bread; wet feet and wet ground to sleep on. Mud to wade through, swollen creaks to ford, muddy springs and a thousand other discomforts attended the rain. Cold winds, blowing the rain in men's faces, increased the misery. Mud was often so deep as to submerge the horses and mules and it was necessary for one man or more to extricate another from the mud holes in the road. Night marching was attended with additional discomforts and dangers, such as falling off bridges, stumbling into ditches, tearing the face and injuring the eyes against bushes and projecting limbs of trees and getting separated from one's own company and getting hopelessly lost and obtaining no sympathy. Very few men had comfortable or fitting shoes and fewer had socks and, as a consequence, the suffering from bruised and inflamed feet was terrible. It was a common practice, on long marches, for men to take off their shoes and carry them in their hands or swung over the shoulder. Bloody footprints in the snow were not unknown to the soldiers of the Army of West Virginia.

In the Franco-Prussian War (1870-1871) the Prussian Guard Corps left the Rhine on August 3rd 1870 and reached Paris on September 19th, fighting two battles on the way. They had started with about 30,000 men and finished with 9,000. When the battle casualties were deducted from the original number it was estimated that the Corps had lost about 12,650 men from fatigue and exposure in 47 days.

Several arduous marches from Kabul to Kandahar in Afghanistan, and some in the opposite direction, were completed by British and native troops in the nineteenth century. One such march was in 1880 when the British government dispatched a force of 10,000 infantry, 11,000 cavalry horses and other animals, and 8,000 camp followers, under General (later Lord) Sir Frederick Roberts, to the relief of the Southern Afghanistan Field Force in Kandahar.

The march was uneventful as far as interference by the enemy was concerned, but it was a great physical feat on the part of man and beast and a triumph of organisation, especially as regards supply, which was almost entirely local, and had to be obtained and distributed daily in a far from prolific and distinctly hostile country.

The British infantry included the 72nd and 92nd Highlanders and the 2/60th Rifles and they were fortunate that in not one single instance during the march did a single soldier or follower fail to receive his rations. Trees on the line of march were almost non-existent and except where spare timber could be obtained from villagers, the only firewood consisted of the roots of shrubs which had to be laboriously excavated. After the first few days' marches, water became a difficulty and was only found at considerable intervals, which made it difficult to keep to an average length for the day's march.

The climate was very trying owing to the extreme variations of temperature, amounting to as much as 80 degrees in 24 hours. The days were hot all the way and got hotter as the march progressed, Kandahar being about 3,500 feet above sea level and Kabul almost 6,000.On some nights the temperature fell nearly to freezing-point and by day reached 110 degrees in the shade. There were constant sandstorms and, of course, suffocating dust raised by the column. The column reached Kandahar after a march of 23 days in which 326 miles had been accomplished. Five soldiers and six followers died on the march, all from illness and none from enemy action.

During the Boer War (1899-1902) and the period of unrest which followed it, hundreds of miles of marching were completed by infantry battalions of the British Empire in South Africa. Two battalions of the Northumberland Fusiliers were particularly busy - in just under a month the 1st Battalion covered 310 miles, the rate varying between 4 and 18 daily. So much marching about was there by this battalion with the object of relieving every one who might be in distress from the Boers, that they became known as the 'Salvation Army' and 'Methuen's Mudcrushers'. The 2nd Battalion, in its turn, marched 265½ miles in three weeks, the day's total varying between 4 and 22. In fifteen consecutive days

On the march in India circa 1897. Note that troops were allowed to smoke pipes whilst marching At Ease

the battalion marched 234½ miles, an average of about 15½ miles a day - a striking achievement when it is remembered that during this period the men were often down to half-rations, snatching food and sleep whenever time allowed, and that each man carried a weight of arms, equipment, ammunition, necessaries, and blanket or greatcoat, from 35 to 40lbs. Despite weariness and sore feet - the soles of the boots were worn down to the thickness of brown paper - the men stuck to their task with unflagging determination. Short though a distance of, say, four miles in a day looks in print it must not be forgotten that many of these marches, because of the nature of the ground, required as much effort to complete as ten miles or more on a level surface. One soldier wrote:

> It was kopjes and kloofs, kloofs and kopjes, the whole time, drops of 400 feet and climbs of 500 feet, so that the five miles passed lightly over by the straight-flying crow, lengthened themselves out into the 12 to 15 for the less mobile, perspiring, foot-slogging, crag-hopping [Tommy] Atkins, particularly when his company happened to be one of the two forming the long, widely-extended line of beaters that stretched from north to south of the long mountain range, and was known as the advanced guard.

One particular day brought a march of exceptional severity - a steady drive through blinding, choking clouds of dust raised by a strong head wind:

> Just had to put down our heads and plough through it for 14 of the longest miles ever travelled - mostly over burnt veldt and dusty road. Arrived about 4.30 pm. at Woolfaard's farm in most deplorable condition. Eyes like well-cooked chops - black outside and blood-red in; faces grimy, hair full of dust, footsore, thirsty and dog-tired. May we never put in such another day!

Yet at 3 o'clock next morning they were on the march again - not amidst heat and dust, but against a high, chill wind which cut into all ranks like a new-set razor. The Commanding Officer of the 2nd Battalion issued regimental orders congratulating the non-commissioned officers and men for 'sticking to a very trying march under difficult circumstances' and the Major-General commanding the column in which the battalion had marched, issued a special order, in which he said:

> I congratulate the troops of the Column upon what they have accomplished so far in this difficult and forced march after an active and clever enemy. Great distances have been got over day by day without waiting for needful food and drink, and in the face of abominable wind and blinding dust. Extreme difficulties have been got over with guns weighing seven tons apiece, and the transport of the Force has been kept going to a degree that beats anything I have seen yet in three wars in South Africa.

Two days later another order was promulgated to the effect that a message had been received from Lord Kitchener, the Chief of Staff, who had expressed his appreciation of the very good marching of the men under great difficulties. Rudyard Kipling, the 'Soldier's Poet' expressed many of the sentiments felt by the sweating foot soldier on the march. In the poem *Route Marchin'*, when he describes a battalion 'marchin' on relief over Injia's sunny plains' he speaks of the daily routine carried out every day:

> At half-past five's Revelly, an' our
>   tents they down must come,
> Like a lot of button mushrooms when
>   you pick 'em up at home.
> But it's over in a minute, an' at six
>   the column starts,
> While the women and the kiddies sit an'
>   shiver in the carts.

Oh, then it's open order, an' we lights
     our pipes an' sings,
An' we talks about our rations an' a
     lot of other things,
An' we think o' friends in England, an'
     we wonders what they're at,
An' 'ow they would admire for to hear
     us sling the *bat*.[2]

Kipling knew some of the tricks employed by the experienced soldier to ease the pain of marching when he wrote:

So 'ark an' 'eed, you rookies, which is
     always grumblin' sore,
There's worser things than marchin' from
     Umballa to Cawnpore;
An' if your 'eels are blistered an' they
     feels to 'urt like 'ell,
You drop some tallow in your socks an'
     that will make 'em well.

He could also have been speaking of the exploits of the 1st and 2nd Battalions of the Northumberland Fusiliers on their long marches during the Boer War when he wrote:

We're foot-slog-slog-slog-sloggin' over Africa -
Foot-foot-foot-foot-sloggin' over Africa -
(Boots-boots-boots-boots-movin' up and down again!)
There's no discharge in the war!

Seven-six-eleven-five-nine-an'-twenty mile today -
Four-eleven-seventeen-thirty-two the day before -
(Boots-boots-boots-boots-moving' up and down again!)
There's no discharge in the war!

---

[2] *Bat* is Urdu for 'language'. The British soldier has always picked up a smattering of the language of the countries in which he has served.

He went on to advise the soldier not to watch the boots of the men in front of him, moving up and down and up and down but to try and think of something else or even count the number of bullets in the bandoliers around him, and stop himself from going mad.

The first crossing of the Tugela River by Lyttleton's Brigade 1900

Another military force which has always prided itself on its marching ability is the French Foreign Legion. In the years leading up to the outbreak of the First World War the trained legionnaire was expected to march, in a day, at least forty kilometres in training, on manoeuvres and in wartime. He was able to march that distance, day by day, without interruption, without a rest day, for weeks on end. Several times every week the men had to make practice marches over a distance of at least 24 kilometres, with full equipment, at the Legion's pace of five kilometres per hour. The only object of the practice marches was to teach the recruits steady quick marching. They neither ended with a small manoeuvre, nor did they have exercises such as scouting, or exploring the country by means of patrols - they just tramped forward to fulfil a specific task. The 'marches militaires', as the practice marches were called, usually commenced at midday, when the sun was at its hottest in Sidi-bel-Abbes, after a hard morning's drill. On one of the military roads which branched off from the depot in all directions, the march went on until the twelfth kilometre stone was reached, and then the men marched back again.

On the march a legionnaire could carry his rifle as he pleased, either shouldered or by the sling, whichever was the more comfortable for him; he could take off his knapsack if it hurt him and carry it by the straps from his hand. He was not ordered to unbutton his coat nor to close it. The officers did not worry the men with paltry orders and they were allowed to sing or smoke as they pleased. Unlike the British Green Jackets in the previous century, when there was a large puddle in the road or when one side of the road was stony, the column turned off on its own accord and marched where the road was best.

In the course of a whole-day march not a single word was heard from the officers, and no orders, except the short whistle signals which meant 'Column, Halt!' and 'Column, Forward March!' As soon as the signal was heard for the column to halt the front ranks formed to their front without orders, and each man sat or laid down during the halt as it suited him best. The marches were regulated by one principle: 'March as you like, with crooked back or toes turned in, if you think that nice or better, but - March!'

It was always being drummed into the men that they were intended for nothing else in the world but for marching. If they suffered pangs of hunger or thirst parched their tongues, that was considered their bad luck but no sort of reason for them *not* marching on. They might be tired, completely exhausted, but they were to keep going. If feet were bleeding and the soles burned like fire, the marching pace was not allowed to slacken. The greatest crime was to fall out on the march. When they could walk no more they were expected to crawl forward. It was a merciless system but seemed to create wonderful fighting men.

Marching was not made any simpler by the sheer burden of the uniform and equipment. The legionnaire marched with an equipment called *tenue de campagne d'Afrique*. He wore splendid laced boots, white duck trousers held together at the ankles by means of leather gaiters, and a heavy blue greatcoat. The coat was put on over the shirt, without any jacket, and its tails were buttoned back behind so that the thighs and knees were left free and an unhindered pace made possible. Around the waist was the *ceinture*, a blue sash, about four metres long, of fine woollen cloth, which not only gave the body firm support but also served as a tropical belt, considered indispensable in the sudden changes of temperature in Africa, where the hot day is followed by an icy cold night. The red képi had a white cover and, as further protection against the sun, a thin linen neck-cloth was buttoned on to the képi, covering the neck, ears and cheeks. There were few cases of sunstroke in the Legion because of this precaution.

The legionnaire carried a rifle and bayonet, two hundred to four hundred cartridges, a cartridge pouch and knapsack, and the *sac*. This kind of knapsack was made of black varnished canvas with a complicated system of straps and had hardly any weight of its own. On the march it contained two complete uniforms, linen and polishing cloths. Tent canvas and a blanket were strapped around the knapsack in a long roll, with collapsible tent-pegs stuck in at the side. On the top was fastened a messtin and fuel for the bivouac fire. In addition, each man carried one of the company saucepans or pioneer's implements. Knapsack, weapons and equipment altogether weighed almost 50kgs and it was claimed that no soldier of any other army carried such a load.

With this kit the legionnaire marched over sand under a burning sun, on very scanty rations. In barracks he got a cup of black coffee at reveille. At 10 am. he got his forenoon soup, at about 5 pm. his afternoon soup. In the soup meat, with all sorts of vegetables, was boiled, carrots and potatoes and suchlike. French military bread was issued with the soup, a grey kind of bread which was easily digested, undoubtedly nutritious, sufficient and palatable. On the march the meat ration was omitted and food consisted almost entirely of rice and macaroni. As a substitute for the bread the troops were served with a kind of hard ship's biscuit. Marching always commenced in the early hours after midnight. It then went on uninterruptedly, with the hourly halts for rest of five minutes, until the journey had been accomplished.

Although the development of the railways had reduced the distances to be marched by infantry on 'change of station' pro-grammes, circumstances dictated that long marches had still to be carried out during the times of war. In August 1914, for example, the soldiers of the German First and Second Armies covered 300 miles between their railheads on the Belgian border and the limit of their advance on the River Marne. The men of general von Kluck's First Army, on the outer flank of the wheeling German armies, marched up to thirty miles a day, and units of the British Expeditionary Force, falling back before them, had to cover similar distances. One participant on the British side described how some marches took on an almost dreamlike quality:

> Of the rest of the night I have no clear recollection;
> it remains in my mind as a blurred nightmare, in
> which shadowy figures slept as they rode or slept as
> they walked, in which phantom teams halted in
> sleep; there stretched for miles a ghostly stream of
> men and in which the will more than ever wrestled
> with the desire to sleep.

A young conscript, serving with the German 113th Infantry Regiment, had a similar memory:

> We slogged on, living, as it were, in a coma, often
> sleeping while we marched, and when the column
> came to a sudden halt we ran with our noses against
> the billy-cans of the men in front of us.

Although the railways did not connect all military stations in India, some did but this did not stop the Army using 'change of station' marches as rigorous training exercises. In 1926, for example, the 1st Battalion of the King's Royal Rifle Corps undertook a march from Rawalpindi to Razmak. Each day's distance was chronicled and the following table gives some indication of the standards expected of British infantry during that period:

Day	Miles marched
1st	12
2nd	15
3rd	10
4th	11½
5	8
6	Rest
7	16
8	15
9	Rest
10	17½
11 days	14 miles
12	12
13	16
14	20
15	Rest
16	14
17	13
18	19½
19	12
20	15
20 days	240½ miles

The longest march in military history was the famous Long March of the Chinese Communists in 1934-35. In 368 days, of which 268 days were days of movement, from October of one year to October of the next, their force of 90,000 men, women and children, covered 6,000 miles (9650 kilometres) from Kiangsi to Yenan in Shensi via Yünan. They crossed eighteen mountain ranges and six major rivers and lost all but 22,000 of their number in continual rearguard actions against nationalist Kuo-min-tang forces.

In the 1930s much discussion and thought centred on the possible role of infantry in any future wars. Whilst some prophesied that battlefield tactics and strategies would be a continuation of those in the First World War - feverish movements of infantry, assisted by tanks, culminating in both sides digging in to preserve ground won - others were more far-sighted. Captain Liddell-Hart, of the British Army, whose opinions set him far apart from those responsible for future military planning in the War Office, but whose opinions were valued (and later implemented, with considerable success) by high-ranking officers in the German Reichswehr, said, in a lecture he gave in 1932 that:

> In a motorised world the marching soldier on the road was a relic from the past....For strategic movement....it is pure commonsense that men in motors can reach a spot before men who march. They can also arrive in greater numbers - so long as one provides sufficient vehicles.

By the time the Second World War started motor transport was often available in sufficient numbers to reduce the distances marched by soldiers behind the battlefield but, once hostilities broke out, the infantry were back on their feet again. During the Polish campaign of 1939 and again, in the French campaign the following spring, the German armoured forces broke through opposition and raced ahead, cutting off large and scattered formations of the enemy. It was, however, the slowly moving German infantry, mainly equipped with horse transport, marching for hundreds of miles, who secured the ground freed by their armour, subjugated any defended localities and captured the remnants of enemy formations broken up by the swift panzer thrusts.

This strategy was continued when the German offensive, codenamed *Barbarossa*, struck the Soviet Union in 1941. The war diaries of German infantry divisions bear testimony that thousands of soldiers marched over 700 miles in that year alone, across hot, dusty plains, then through heavy rain and mud and, later in the year, along roads rendered nearly impassable because of snow and slush (with the ever-present dangers of frostbite and gangrene). The war diary of the 112th Division recalled that:

> Even though the division had a good deal of experience in poor road conditions, what was now demanded of it vastly exceeded anything known in the past. The completely sodden forest paths, the area of swampy marsh and the sticky clay on open ground simply defy description....The infantry regiments had spread out into unendingly long columns: the heavy vehicles were unable to keep up and had to be manhandled along.

In the retreat of the British Army through Burma in 1942 it was the experience of many men to fall asleep on the march, their desire for rest proving stronger than their instinct for self-preservation. They would fight off sleep while maintaining a fast pace but eventually weariness would cause them to close their eyes and veer off the path. It was possible for a man to collapse and lie where he was in this condition but if he was 'fortunate' he might walk into a tree or other vegetation or stumble over a root or uneven ground and bring himself to life. If these events did not happen or his comrades failed to notice him fall or veer off the path it was possible for the men, especially if they were in the rear of a column, to become lost or fall victim to the pursuing enemy.

Marching at night, combined with patrolling, rearguard actions, reconnaissance and sometimes digging defensive positions all combined to cause exhaustion in the retreating columns. At halts during the night movements some of the officers and men were kept standing, to watch that men did not stray away or remain recumbent when the time for moving came again. The little time available for rest was sometimes occupied in digging trenches which were abandoned when the orders came to resume the retreat.

On the last day of a 900 mile retreat Field Marshal William Slim and other officers watched the rearguard of the Burma Army march painfully into India. The men were described as looking like scarecrows, with ragged uniforms and cracked boots. All of them - British, Indian and Gurkha - looked thin and under nourished but they still carried their arms and kept ranks and tried to straighten their backs when they saw the high-ranking officers standing beside the road watching their progress.

About this time of low military morale General Archibald Wavell wrote to the War Office and told them that until Britain had once again soldiers capable of marching 20 to 30 miles a day for days running and missing their full rations every second or third day, and whose first idea was to push forward and engage the enemy at every opportunity, whatever the difficulties and odds, the morale and reputation of the fighting forces and the country behind them would never be recovered.

In 1943 Colonel (later General) Orde Wingate's Chindits seemed to give the lie to General Wavell's opinion of the British infantryman of the time. Wingate's men were older than the average foot soldier - mainly between the ages of 28 and 35 - and marched from their base in India into Japanese-held Burma. They moved into the jungle, mainly at night - the period in which the Japanese soldier had always seemed to be at home.

Elephants carried mortars and heavy machine-guns and other loads were carried by the men, mules and in carts pulled by buffaloes and oxen. Because of the difficult terrain they could only manage to move a mere mile in a whole night but sometimes, as the tracks became easier they could slog 18 to 20 miles. The River Chindwin, broad and fast-flowing, was crossed at night despite the attentions of enemy patrols and lookouts. The men could sometimes scarce keep their eyelids open because in the daylight, when they might hope for a rest, they were kept busy with military tasks or plagued by insects or flies. Air supply enabled them to keep going ever further into the jungle.

The Japanese were then aware of their presence and had a force of over 15,000 men to oppose them. As Wingate had noted that his men were no longer capable of continuing their advance because of sheer exhaustion, he split the force into several groups and instructed them to make their way back into India.

Day after day they marched across the hills, as their route crossed the 'grain' of the country and their path came to resemble a switchback of hills and valleys. Their thoughts were centred on solid, rich food and they were tortured by a craving for sugar. They experimented with grass and berries, as they did not always know what to eat, sometimes with dire results. Some of the columns marched 1,300 miles in 88 days, across terrible country and some shed nearly all their equipment, save their clothing, weapons and ammunition. They were emaciated, with a body loss, on average, of about a third of their original weight. Although by this time the Japanese were always snapping at their heels the Chindits did not always regard them as their chief enemy. Hunger and extreme fatigue were their prime considerations. They became lousy and scratched their skinny bodies, covered with bites and sores, all the time. Many got foot-rot, boots gave out and some marched with bare feet, tortured by thorny undergrowth and sharp grass-stems. They existed on a handful of rice apiece, flavoured with any fragments of food left in their rotting haversacks or pockets.

When they re-crossed the Chindwin the original 3,000 had shrunk to 2,182. Of these only about 600 were fit for further active soldiering, and many died shortly after they had reached India, as a result of the privations they had suffered.

In the fighting in New Guinea, Guam, New Britain and on the Assam Front in the war against Japan, soldiers of the Allied armies described the awful terrain through which they had to march. In mountainous jungles they sweated and slipped through deep puddles and clinging mud, their hearts pounding from their exertions. When they had the chance to rest in was often in puddles, panting and steaming and wet through. One soldier wrote that he found the handle of his machine-gun on his shoulder, his pack and shovel, canteens, bayonet and machete all stuck out at right angles and caught up on the underbrush like so many grappling hooks. After straining, sweating and swearing he only freed himself by making a despairing lunge, which tired him out still further, lathered him with more stinging sweat and caused him to sprawl headlong on to the path, grazing his hands and face. The flies and mosquitoes sucked the blood from his skin which was itching, burning and caked with sweat and dust. The moist humidity of the jungle was overpowering, causing yet more sweat to start from every pore at the slightest exertion and pour down the body, saturating everything. The chests, stomachs, groins and armpits of the troops stank with jungle rot and fungus infection ate away at their feet.

Even in the more normal environment of Europe it was possible for men to be nearly at the end of their tether through sheer fatigue and loss of sleep. Men coming away from the hell of the Cassino battle were seen to be marching mechanically, their feet scarcely leaving the ground, stumbling over the slightest bump in the ground, their eyes half-closed, staring straight ahead but not seeing anything. Their past training caused them to keep their positions in the columns and lines, relying on the men in front to choose their route for them and as the troops in front halted those following them collided with the equipment and arms of their comrades, causing some to be shocked awake. Some were in pain, from minor wounds, aching limbs and lacerated feet, some actually asleep, others vomiting but they all managed to somehow keep the cadence of the march going - left, right, left, right - in the sub-conscious rhythm hammered into them in the far-off parade grounds or long, cool, leafy roads during springtime route marches years before.

Observers have described the spectacle of long lines of British infantry plodding steadily up a dusty French road towards the front after the landings in Normandy in 1944. The men marched in single file along both sides of the road, heads bent down against the heavy weight of the heavy loads piled on their backs, armed to the teeth and trying to keep step with their comrades in front although this was not insisted upon in times of war. They moved slowly, sweat running down their faces, enamel mugs swinging from their packs or waistbelts, never looking back and hardly ever noticing what was on both sides of the road. They just stared straight ahead or down at the roughness of the road before them. All the while tanks, jeeps, lorries, artillery and other traffic went crowding by, smothering the infantry in clouds of dust which, except for the occasional shouted curse, they did not seem to notice but spat out the grit from their mouths and cleared their nasal passages noisily.

Any soldier who has experienced such marching will remember those half-forgotten moments when the future faded away and all that was left was the grinding left, right, left and the imperative urge to keep up with comrades and not fall by the wayside.

Miles away, in the east, the Soviet Army recorded its greatest advance of the Second World War when its infantry marched a total of 500 kilometres in the Vislo-Odersk offensive and, the following year, in the closing stages of the war, the record was again broken when their troops marched nearly 800 kilometres against the Japanese in Manchuria.

By the summer of 1944 the tide of battle had turned against the Japanese and the ordinary run-of-the-mill British infantry had stood and fought and, as the enemy broke and retreated, they proceeded to drive him out of Burma.

The distances they had to cover, the awful country to be crossed and savage rains made a hell for the infantry of both sides. One particular stretch of the Tiddim trail was given the name of 'The Chocolate Staircase'. It climbed 3,000 feet in seven miles, with scores of hairpin bends and an average gradient of one in twelve. As its surface was earth the thousands of men and animals who had worked their way up had churned it into brown, ankle-deep, clinging mud. The mountainside was constantly being washed away by torrential rains, making progress that more dangerous as masses of earth were loosened, threatening to bury whole columns of men, mules and material at a time. After such a fall the men would have to salvage picks and shovels from the mud and, still weighed down with equipment and exhaustion, set to clear the track again. There was more than one 'Chocolate Staircase' to be encountered along the march through Burma and even these were considered Heaven when a change of route meant hacking away at dense undergrowth, clinging vegetation and waterlogged ground all on a gradient which meant that the boots of the man in front threatened to mash the face of anybody following.

From diaries kept by some of those involved it is possible to guess what the individual soldier experienced during the advance in Burma, especially those marching forward 'at the bleedin' sharp end'. The marches went on for weeks at a time, nearly always through mountainous, trackless jungle. Day after day the routine never varied: march, stop, dig-in, march, patrol, stand-to, stand-down, short rest, if one was lucky, stand-to, move off. A long, straggling file of sweating men and mules, covered with stinging dust or clinging mud. When the column moved out of the jungle into comparitively open country, of scrub or bare landscape, the way ahead was still not easy, marching down dry river courses, stumbling over rocks and fallen trees, always short of water. Sometimes it was possible to dig in the sand of a river bed and find a muddy liquid which served, after treatment, as a means to brew tea or sponge the muzzles of the mules. Tea was the stand-by throughout the campaign. Each section carried a battered, blackened jam tin, with a makeshift wire handle in which tea was prepared whenever the time was suitable. There was never a quarrel about who carried the 'makings' for a drink of tea but many arguments as to whose turn it was to carry the Bren light machine gun or spare magazines. The mules sometimes staggered under the amount of baggage they carried but the loads were rarely excessive - after all, if the mules died their baggage would have to be subdivided between the sections or platoons. Water and reserve ammunition was carried by the mules, in bulk panniers. Everything else was carried by the men - weapons, half a blanket each, toilet articles, a tin of bully and hard biscuits, a pair of messtins and other necessaries.

On one occasion, during the same Burma campaign of 1944 a battalion of a British county regiment was sent out into rocky, hilly country, interspersed with small villages, mango groves and scrub desert. The march lasted three weeks. Sometimes the men were so exhausted they fell asleep on their feet but kept marching. They went on, blindly following the man in front. When the column stopped ahead, men would bump into those in front, like shunting trucks on a railway siding.

After the initial pain and throbbing in their feet the soldier hardly noticed them because he ached all over. Officers and sergeants had to raise their voices to awaken their men and get them to deploy or dig in at such and such a position. The buzz of insects helped to lull them to sleep and when an order to halt came or if the column stopped of its own volition some would crumple to the ground, hard though it might be, and sleep like infants until kicked into wakefulness.

If the column stopped for any length of time sentries would be posted and to ensure security they would be posted in pairs or even threes to punch each other awake if they happened to doze.

Eventually the scrub turned to desert country and finally a long steep rise towards the crest of a high hill and their agonies increased as they bent forward with fatigue and chest pains and their breathing became more laboured from their exertions. They expected a breeze but the air on that mountainside was oven hot and still and the sun beat down from a cloudless sky.

There was another side to the coin. The positions of the opposing armies had more than reversed. The condition of the retreating British troops at the beginning of the Burma campaign had been appalling enough but after General Mutaguchi's XVth Army's much-trumpeted 'March to Delhi' had been halted and then thrown back, his troops, in turn, had to endure many privations, made worse by the failure of his supply trains to deliver food and ammunition and the steady and unrelenting pressure of his pursuers. The Japanese were forced to retreat.

One account speaks of the state of shattered divisions of infantry falling back along mountain roads, many without weapons, using sticks to help them on their way and clutching their rice tins. They stumbled painfully through the torrential rain. Wounded were carried by their comrades or jolted painfully along on horse-drawn sledges. The more seriously wounded were abandoned to die by the sides of the tracks. The survivors struggled on, some suffering from untended wounds, all frantic with hunger and many racked by malaria and dysentery.

After the Second World War the armies of the victors reverted back to their ordinary peace-time training. After the harrowing experiences of infantry warfare the training became more realistic and, for a time, even tougher than the pre-war programmes, to ready their men for what might lie ahead.

Infantry training was put to the test in wars in Malaya and Indo-China but it was in Vietnam in the 1960s that the American foot soldier faced the ultimate examination of his ability to cope with appalling conditions of a hostile environment, in every sense of the word, with, sometimes, appalling weather conditions.

Although the United States Army enjoyed tactical mobility unprecedented in the history of war, in the shape of a wide range of helicopters available to transport stores, including ammunition and rations, to supply supporting fire and assisting units in the evacuation of casualties, the soldier on the ground had to walk. He bore staggering amounts of kit on his back and secured to his person by a plethora of straps and other attachments. To prepare him for his ordeal the training at the depots at home was harsh and sometimes unfeeling.

One victim of this type of training remembered that what he recalled most vividly was the close order drill staged on an asphalt square that was melting under a blazing sun, so much so that his boots often stuck to the blisters of asphalt. His instructors scourged the squad with all sorts of insults and obscene name-calling. Their reason for acting in such a manner was based on their belief that if a man could not take being sworn at and 'having his arse kicked' he was not fit to be a US Marine nor could he ever be relied upon to withstand the rigours of combat. As a result the men worked hard at their drill and submitted to all kinds of moral and physical indignity to prove to their instructors that 'they could take it'.

If a man was fit enough to pass the course and be posted to a fighting outfit he had every chance to partake in advanced courses a couple of years later. Here he would be exposed to endurance training which could take several forms. The worst was based on a hill-running exercise which called for squads, wearing the inevitable American full marching order, marching over a range of hills at least twice a week. Dozens of men sometimes collapsed on these runs. One young soldier, obviously overweight, collapsed unconscious against a tree stump. A sergeant ran over to him, swearing abuse and tried to yank him to his feet by shaking him by his collar, threatening him with all sorts of punishment if he did not resume his run.

The Marine remembered the sun beating down on a file of soldiers in camouflaged uniform, bent down under unbearable loads. The thick dust raised by the tramping boots clung to their uniforms stained by sweat, and streamed down their faces and inside their shirts like rivers of mud. As the men ran and marched their ears were assailed by the clink of ironmongery in the shape of messtins, bayonet scabbards and the metal fitments of their rifle slings. Their heads ached from the weight of their heavy helmets. Despite every effort to keep station the men ran into the backs of those in front or were trodden on from the rear as the column behaved like a concertina, first closing up then opening out as the varying speeds of the men and their differing states of fatigue affected the pace.

At the start the column moved regularly at an easy pace, sometimes practically marking time to allow those at the rear to catch up. Then the pace quickened, seemingly of its own volition, causing those behind to run to keep their station, castigated by their instructors, who called them all sorts of names, accusing them of cowardice, gutlessness and even being guilty of sexually deviant behaviour because they had lost station in the column. Worse, as the men in front were enjoying a five minute break at the hour, lying on the cool grass, enjoying a few puffs of a cigarette, those lagging behind arrived in time for the order 'Fall in, fall in, get back on the road!' so missing that heavenly break in marching.

If training was tough, action was a thousand times worse. If a soldier fell out on a training march the very worst that could happen was a spell in the 'stockade' but in Vietnam there was always the danger of stepping on a land mine or being caught alone by a savage enemy.

Many gripping accounts exist of patrol actions carried out by the 'Grunts' (a fitting word, not needing explanation) of infantry battalions in the same theatre of war. Stripped of their obvious exaggerations the truth comes through with stunning clarity. One man found that the weight of his full equipment, 'mostly a rucksack weighing about 100lbs' (45 kgs) made it harder to walk down mountains than to climb up them. The route went up over hills, over rocks and water. The gradient was sometimes such that progress was only possible by hauling oneself up, hand-over-hand through the tangled roots of trees. If they waited for the column in front to struggle down a hill, some soldiers fell asleep, leaning against trees. They dare not sit down as it was sometimes impossible to stand up again, unaided. There were only two men in one company who could heave on a rucksack standing up. The usual practice for the others was to remove the sack whilst facing a tree. In that way it was easier to put the sack on when sitting on the ground, then grab the tree to heave the body upright again.

At the end of a breathless, exhausting day's struggling through the jungle it was not unknown for a command to be relayed from headquarters, many miles away, to climb a nearby feature hundreds of feet high, in thick vegetation to see if any of the enemy were encamped there. The hills were always steep and many times the feet of a man would be level with the sweating face of the soldier following. The unit would sometimes see men from other platoons in front, slumped semi-conscious by the side of the track. Officers and NCOs, despite their own weariness, would try to physically force the men to their feet and, if they could not, their rucksacks and weapons would be taken from them, leaving them helpless and hungry behind, to catch up if they could. More often than not the stragglers would eventually stumble in to rejoin their platoons, sometimes hours later.

After a man had reached the top of a steep hill he looked as if he had just climbed out of a swimming pool because he was wet and salty from sweat. At the end of the day the soldiers could barely put one foot in front of the other. One had jungle rot on his hands so bad that the only way he could carry his rifle was to cradle it in the bend of his arms, with his hands held up, out of harm's way, in front of his face. His hands were sore and burning, as were his feet.

The British Falklands campaign of 1982 gave those journal-
ists allowed to accompany some of the troops the opportunity of
witnessing infantry on the march and in action. Unfortunately,
because of their inexperience in matters military and their tendency
to believe whatever was told them by the participating soldiery
they went completely 'over the top' in some of their accounts.
Much footage was given to a word 'yomping' which was said to be
Marine slang for a long march under heavy kit. In Parachute
language it was known as 'tabbing'.

The march across the Falklands was described as 'epic' and
one chronicler estimated the weight of a Royal Marine Commando
pack and equipment as a colossal 120lbs. A 40-mile march (or
'yomp') included the hazards of wading ankle-deep in marshland,
struggling across rivers and hauling themselves up mountains at
night, amidst sleet, snow and torrential rain. Refuge was sometimes
taken in farm buildings where, after boots and sleeping bags (save
the mark!) had been dried, it was possible to rest. Meals (known as
'scran' to the Falklands veterans) were sometimes eaten cold to
avoid the giveaway light of a hexamine cooking stove.

The commanding officer of 45 Commando, before the
advance, reminded them that their fathers had walked from
Normandy to Berlin so a march to Stanley should be no great
problem. This particular account ended with a remark ascribed to
a senior officer of the expedition that the only difference between
his troops and Hannibal was that his men had walked all the way
and the Carthaginian commander had elephants.

Another journalist, indulging in the same tenor of report-
ing, described the march between the beach-head at San Carlos and
the ring of Argentine positions around Port Stanley - forty miles
of desolate country in only five days - as 'a prodigious feat'. After
squelching through marshes the canvas webbing stiffened and
shrank on their bodies and their hair hung matted 'on their skulls'.

A more restrained account of the same operation described
how lead units of the 3rd Battalion the Parachute Regiment,
wearing fighting order only, left Port San Carlos, virtually at the
trot, heading for Teal Inlet, about thirty miles away as the crow
flies. By nightfall they were making their way across inhospitable

countryside of foot-hugging peat bog, freezing streams and ankle-breaking stone slides, literally rivers of rock, that wandered down just about every hillside in the Falklands. One of the participants said that it was like the blind following the blind. It was so dark that not many men could be seen ahead. When a man fell into a hole those following could not avoid him as they had not seen him fall, so they tumbled down on top of him, sometimes causing injuries to themselves or the unfortunate(s) below them.

The more one reads of such experiences the more one realises that nothing really changes in life (or war). Despite the rate of human progress battle strips away all the trimmings and it is easy to imagine the Roman legionary suffering the same discomfort in some campaign in Northern Europe so many years ago as his twentieth century counterparts.

Amidst growing complaints of the unsuitability of the British ankle boot used by most troops in the Falklands campaign, despite the fact that it had been well and truly tested in hundreds of campaigns for over eighty years, in terrain vastly more uncomfortable than that experienced in the Falklands, its death sentence was inevitable. Some accounts spoke glowingly of the footwear worn by the Argentine troops - made of good leather, with stout soles and high laced uppers - and, as a result the boot, combat, high (BCH), already being tested, became a general issue to British troops. Whether this will be satisfactory, time will tell.

It is somewhat ironic that with all the latest technological advances made in weaponry for armies the basic requirement of a suitable and comfortable item of infantry clothing is still a subject for experiment and argument.

Chapter Eight

Transport of Infantry

The ability to move warriors as quickly as possible to a place from which to launch an attack on an enemy has always been a predominant factor in the waging of war.

The first men probably used chopped-down tree trunks to carry them across rivers and Hannibal, using the same system, had rafts constructed to ferry his troops, elephants, horses and stores across wide rivers on his transalpine expedition against the Romans.

Early records depict the use of various kinds of transport for carrying infantry into battle. An early Icelandic manuscript shows an ungainly-looking waggon, with castellated sides, being drawn by a single horse. There are a dozen or so warriors crowded in the cart. They are wearing chain-mail and carry shields and some are clutching long spears. The ground in the illustration appears uneven and the combined weight of waggon and troops appears too much for one horse to pull along. Under the circumstances it is unlikely that such a conveyance would have been generally used in time of war.

The Bayeux tapestry pictures the use of small sailing ships for the conveyance of an army to the beaches. A picture in the *Diebold Schilling Amtliche Chronik* of the mid-fifteenth century shows a fleet of small rowing boats on a river, en route to battle. The boats are loaded to the gunwales with Swiss soldiers. In one vessel armour-clad men-at-arms are armed with pikes and cross-bows. About ten men are using oars. A wooden mantelet in the stern protects men tending at least five heavy cannon, the barrels of which protrude from openings in the shield.

Small boats, barges and a variety of other craft have been used to carry troops into action for centuries - from the Norman invasion of 1066 to the Normandy landings of 1944, Salerno, Anzio, Korea and the Falklands, as well as countless smaller raids by armed men using canoes or similar craft. Once ashore the men, whether they were Vikings, infantry of the line or Commandos, usually marched into action on foot.

Until the second half of the nineteenth century the fighting man generally moved into battle on foot, carrying all his needs for several days. This was understood by everyone who wished to travel to another part of the country and who could not afford to

Artist's impression of a waggon carrying foot soldiers circa 10th century AD (from an early Icelandic manuscript)

travel by coach. *Everybody* walked - armies, grandparents, wives and children, even the families' cattle and pigs - for days, sometimes weeks on end. British troops in India, moreover, were expected to march for hundreds of miles for weeks at a time in a change-of-station operation, from one end of the sub-continent to the other.

In the days before the railways were used for transporting troops and equipment there was no satisfactory method by which fighting men could be carried direct to the battlefield.

Towards the end of the eighteenth century experiments were carried out to find ways of moving forces by means other than marching. In 1796, for example, it was reported in a London newspaper that trials had been made with a carriage for the speedy conveyance of troops. It was a light waggon, designed to carry fifty men with their arms and baggage, drawn by six horses and ridden by two postilions. It was calculated that the conveyance would travel nearly as fast as a stagecoach. The soldiers sat on rows of seats, one banked above the other. Arms and accoutrements were deposited in a long, narrow chest running along the centre of the waggon. Although the test was, apparently, successful such waggons do not seem to have been widely used, least of all in battle.

Experiments were still being carried out in 1798 and the artist Thomas Rowlandson drew a picture depicting a body of Guards en route from London to Portsmouth to embark for Ireland in that year. The Guards are seen riding in various types of horse-drawn transport - coaches, light waggons and experimental military flys (with troops sitting in rows, back to back). It was reported that 1,900 rank and file plus officers, completed this stage of the journey in ten hours.

The problem of getting infantry into action was eventually partially solved by the introduction of mounted infantry or dragoons. These moved forward at speed, dismounted and fought on foot until the main columns of infantry arrived.

Another of the similar experiments carried out involved the use of the newly perfected pedal bicycle. It was first used in England for military purposes and after successful trials had been carried out there, the French adopted the idea wholeheartedly in 1866. So enthusiastically did they embrace this new military concept that they soon caught up with the British and, in fact, set up a new organisation in greater detail.

In 1895 the French Minister of War issued a general order concerning military bicyclists. Their role was three-fold - first and foremost they had to ensure the rapid transmission of orders between headquarters and fighting units, to act singly or in small groups as scouts, or to operate in groups for the purpose of reconnaissance or making a forced march ahead of the main columns. Any French soldier who became proficient in the use of a bicycle went before a board for assessment as a military cyclist. The applicant had to have a good education and a fair knowledge of military topography and be able to ride about forty miles in hilly country in less than six hours and be able to mend or replace the principal parts of his machine. During the final test ride the candidate was told to bring in a report of the country he had traversed or a sketch of some part of it and marks were given according to the intelligence and speed with which he accomplished his mission.

Having passed the board the candidate got a certificate and could, in war or on manoeuvres, be called upon to form part of an impromptu cyclist company for the purpose of making a reconnaissance, a forced march or any other special mission. It was not long before a French officer invented a folding bicycle, capable of being carried on the soldier's back. In manoeuvres it was proved that a cycle detachment was capable of scouting and patrol missions, successfully carrying out turning movements for harassing and pursuing a retreating enemy and for acting in support of cavalry. In both British and French armies the success of the military bicyclist was attributed not so much to the effect of their speed and mobility and the secrecy and silence of their march but because, riding on their bicycles they formed, in the true sense, an ideal mounted infantry. That is to say, infantry which could cover any distance with the speed of cavalry and then act purely as infantry, no matter on what ground or under what circumstances they found themselves placed.

French troops using their portable bicycles for a reconnaissance as mounted infantry circa 1897

It is not difficult to see that being likened to cavalry or dragoons would have been appreciated by members of bicycle detachments and a study of the uniforms of such units in the British Volunteer formations shows that no effort was spared to present a dashing appearance. Cloth gaiters, bandoliers, knee-breeches and crossbelts and so on served to set the men and officers of the bicycle detachments apart from their more plainly uniformed comrades.[1]

---

[1] History has a tendency to sometimes repeat itself. In the first four months of 1988 the Royal Danish Lifeguards carried out a trial with pedal bicycles, involving a company of 120 men. The results were not conclusive and it was decided that, for the time being, bicycles would not be introduced in the army.

During the American Civil War and the Franco-Prussian War vast numbers of troops were carried as near as possible to the scene of action by railway. They were then off-loaded and marched the rest of the way.

It was not until the First World War that mechanical transport came into any use to any extent to provide greater mobility for the foot soldier, notably before the Battle of the Marne when civilian buses, taxicabs and a variety of commercial vehicles were commandeered to take British and French troops forward rapidly to protect Paris from the advancing German armies in 1914.

After the First World War experiments were tried out to cut down the time taken by infantry to reach the battlefield. Various forms of mechanical transport (or troop-carrying vehicles) and aircraft were used and, just before the start of the Second World War, the concept of motorised infantry was launched in Britain. The establishment varied but it was based on the theory that an armoured division, with its tanks, would also include a battalion or so of infantry carried on trucks or TCVs.

The idea was not only taken up more enthusiastically by the German Reichswehr but expanded, with more lorried infantry battalions, some of which were later carried in half-tracked armoured personnel carriers.

In the 1930s the Soviet Red Army experimented with the idea of using forces dropped by parachute to land behind German lines. The German Army, once again, refined the system of airborne forces by adding an element of glider-borne infantry, towed by three-engined JU 52s. These proved their worth in the audacious and successful attack on Belgium's 'impregnable' Fort Eben Emael in the Second World War. Because of appalling losses in the attack on the British-held island of Crete, the idea of glider-borne troops was abandoned by the Germans.

In the meantime, Britain had organised parachute and glider-borne forces and, with similar American formations, used them with great success in the Normandy landings of 1944 and the Rhine Crossing operation the following year.

British infantrymen and, no doubt, their counterparts overseas, have always been ingenious fellows and, following the foot-soldier's adage 'a third-class ride is better than a first-class walk' have made use of a variety of forms of transport to assist their progress.

Although not strictly a case of infantry being transported *to* a battlefield there was a memorable occasion during the Battle of Waterloo in 1815 when men of the Gordon Highlanders, in danger of being caught in a dangerously isolated position by French cavalry, made their way back to the safety of their lines by grasping hold of the stirrups of horses ridden by their countrymen in the Royal Scots Greys.

Other *ad hoc* arrangements for 'hitching a ride' or 'saving boot leather' during the centuries include riding on bullock or horse-drawn waggons, horses, elephants and camels, motor transport of all kinds - motor cycles (solo and combination), motor vans and lorries, civilian, military and captured enemy vehicles (tracked, wheeled or armoured), pedal bicycles and tricycles, even multi-wheeled cycles and so on. All these different forms of transport have played their part in helping the weary infantrymen on their way.

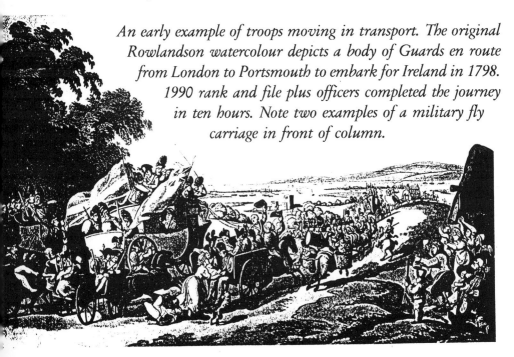

An early example of troops moving in transport. The original Rowlandson watercolour depicts a body of Guards en route from London to Portsmouth to embark for Ireland in 1798. 1990 rank and file plus officers completed the journey in ten hours. Note two examples of a military fly carriage in front of column.

Appendix

A Soldier's Notes on Marching, Drill and Equipment.

1939. Writer enlisted in Grenadier Guards on November 17th on a regular army engagement of 4 years with the Colours and 8 years in the Reserve. Reported to Guards Depot Wing at Chelsea Barracks, London. Posted to Recruits' Reception Squad for two days, awaiting more volunteers to make up a training squad of 24 men. Issued first with ankle boots and anti-gas respirator. Instructed by Trained Soldier how to polish boots correctly - applying polish to leather and rubbing in small circles with spit.

Training squad completed. Started programme of foot drill and weapon training. First taught position of attention and progressing to marching (by means of balance step - slow and quick time). Issued with battledress blouse and trousers; service dress (1914 pattern) with long puttees; canvas drill jacket and trousers (for musketry and fatigues); 1937 pattern webbing equipment; 1908 pattern webbing equipment (for musketry); Short Magazine Lee Enfield rifle with long bayonet; steel helmet, etc. Instructed how to assemble webbing equipment (with tips for shaping pouches, haversack and large valise (back pack) with stiff cardboard or plywood). Shown how to press uniform, including greatcoat under bed blanket. Route marches in service dress and puttees. Firing ranges in battledress uniform and 1937 pattern equipment. Lessons in stripping rifle, Bren light machine gun and 36M grenade.

Ordeal of preparing for kit inspection as per regimental layout - all metal parts burnished, everything that could be cleaned scrubbed white (including cord of rifle pullthrough); urine buckets in barrack rooms shone to mirror brightness, floors and corridors scrubbed and polished, beds in perfect alignment.

Shown by old soldiers how to polish boots and cap badges - a liberal coating of Kiwi on the former ignited for a second or so then extinguished. More polish applied and boned with end of toothbrush, to get rid of the 'pimples' on the leather. Finished off with spit and polish circling, completing the process with a soft cloth (purchased from meagre soldier's pay of two shillings [20 pence] a day from NAAFI (Navy, Army and Air Force Institutes) canteen in barracks). The cap badge was placed in the lid of a boot polish tin, flooded with metal polish and ignited for a short time. Too much heat and the solder joining the badge to its tab would melt. Finished off with issue brush and soft cloth. Back of the badge (and the brass buttons of service dress tunic and greatcoat) rigorously inspected by officers on ceremonial parades. 'Dirty' badges, buttons, rifles, bayonets and webbing equipment (to be carefully blancoed) sometimes resulted in a punishment of Pack Drill on the square during the evenings. Defaulters wore full marching order and carried rifles and were mercilessly drilled by duty drill instructor.

1940. After 10-12 weeks' training writer was posted to Grenadier Guards Training Battalion at Victoria Barracks, Windsor. Here training in heavier weapons - 2-inch and 3-inch mortars, and Vickers medium machine guns, for example - was given, together with ceremonial drill, sentry drill, tactics, map reading and the like. Route marches into the surrounding countryside became the norm and more work on the rifle and machine gun range. Night guards were provided by the battalion on Windsor Castle. Guards detachments marched to the Castle through the streets of Windsor to the sound of drums and fifes.

In June 1940, about the time of the Dunkirk evacuation and the threat of the German invasion, the author asked for and was granted a transfer to the Royal Northumberland Fusiliers, a medium machine gun regiment, as a change from guard duties at Windsor Castle and the like. He joined the regimental depot at Fenham Barracks. There was little marching to glory in Newcastle - the infrequent training marches were leisurely affairs compared to those which were still in the future. One of the chores awarded to the depot troops was the awful job of tending the smoke-producing apparatus to mask the Tyne and shipyards from the Luftwaffe. The smell permeated the denim battledress and equipment and probably brought about a spate of ailments affecting the chests and throats of those participating.

Whilst at the depot all ranks were aroused halfway through the night and ordered to 'stand-to'. Information was sparse but the troops gathered that the expected German invasion had started - the Wehrmacht had, it was said, landed troops in Wales. As they donned their equipment, drew Vickers machine guns from the stores together with boxes of live ammunition in belts and loaded 15 cwt trucks, they had no time to discuss what on earth the Jerry strategy was about. They drove through the night to some high ground overlooking Newcastle and dug in. Came the dawn and they looked down on the sleeping city and worried about the fate of their families when the Germans started their attack. Through the rest of the morning they improved their gun positions and cleared a field of fire for their Vickers machine guns. After dinner (of corned beef between thick 'doorsteps' of bread, and scalding hot tea) they were told to 'stand down', load their weapons onto the trucks and fill in the deep holes they had dug. (It was not until years afterwards that they learned that they had taken part in 'Cromwell' - the anti-invasion operation. The cause of the alarm is still a mystery - some have it that a War Office clerk, practising the transmission of operational orders, had inadvertently sent out the codeword and so launched one of the biggest flaps of the war.)

Posted to 7th Battalion Royal Northumberland Fusiliers in Scotland - a newly-raised machine gun battalion of National Service men with a small cadre of officers and NCOs who had escaped capture of the original 7th Battalion (of the 51st Highland Division) at St. Valery in May 1940. Writer resumed training - route marches, drill, medium machine gun instruction and the rest of a normal military programme.

Manoeuvres and field firing exercises brought the painful experience of 'long carries' of equipment from 15cwt trucks to gun positions. This involved a man shouldering the Vickers MMG, with water-filled jacket, weighing 42½lbs, or its tripod (47lbs) whilst other unfortunate gun-numbers stumbled over rough ground with unwieldy boxes of machine gun belts. Fusiliers also took turns in shouldering the Boys anti-tank rifle, 63½ inches in length, weighing 36lbs, as well as Bren Guns, 2-inch and 3-inch mortars and bombs, together with the normal infantry load of webbing equipment, grenades, rifle and light machine gun ammunition in magazines, and so on.

For a short time the battalion was allotted the responsibility of manning pillboxes and other defensive positions on the coast of Northumberland near Newbiggin-by-the-Sea. No marching was involved nor long carries of machine guns. Trucks dumped sections near their allotted posts and they tried to make themselves comfortable. The author's section occupied a small concrete pillbox, accommodating a First World War naval 6-pounder on a metal base. There was also an American Maxim machine gun with boxes of ammunition and a tool which facilitated the loading of bullets into machine gun belts. Any thoughts that this tool would have been extremely useful back in the battalion were dispelled when it was found that the bullets were not the same calibre as the 0.303 inch Mk VIII streamlined ammunition issued to machine gun battalions. In any case the hand-over of the pillbox and its contents was a very strict procedure, with every item having to be accounted for. The stay on the coast lasted only a few days - marked by one distressing incident when a large spherical mine was seen bobbing about in the sea about five hundred yards out. With the utmost solemnity the author carefully superintended the loading of the Maxim, estimated the range and ordered the No.1 to fire. After a few bursts, expending at least half of the ammunition belt, the mine sank beneath the waves quietly, without the expected explosion. A few days later the author was interviewed by his Commanding Officer and a policeman and asked to account for the wilful destruction of a marker buoy destined to indicate the presence of an underwater obstruction. His explanation was reluctantly excepted.

After periods of training in Scotland and Yorkshire the battalion moved to Northern Ireland, as part of the 59th (Staffordshire) Division. In addition to security duties, battalion, brigade and divisional guards, the Fusiliers engaged in numerous field firing exercises and divisional manoeuvres, with the attendant arduous 'long carries'.

1942. As a result of the boredom and frustration experienced by the men of the Division, a recruiting mission for volunteers for Airborne Forces and Commandos was highly successful and the writer was posted to 1st Battalion Royal Ulster Rifles at Bulford, Wiltshire. This battalion was composed of peacetime Regular Army soldiers and volunteers for airborne duties and was one of three battalions forming the 1st Air-landing (glider-borne) Brigade. Together with two Parachute Brigades and supporting troops the whole constituted the 1st Airborne Division.

Training was intensive, involving regular route marches, boarding and alighting from Hotspur and Horsa gliders, night and day flying and a new experience for the writer - road walks and runs. These consisted of troops wearing full equipment and steel helmets first marching at a quick pace then running, marching and running, sometimes for 8-10 miles at a stretch. The route marches sometimes involved a long march during the day, bivouacking at night and returning by a different route to camp.

Exercises were of the same pattern but, instead of erecting bivouacs, the battalion adopted tactical positions which called for trenches and weapon slits to be dug. The following morning the holes were filled in and the battalion marched back to barracks. On a few occasions the battalion band travelled over from regimental headquarters in Northern Ireland and was available to play the troops back home over the last mile or so - a ceremony which meant a great deal to exhausted men near the end of their tether. It was striking how blistered feet and aching backs were soon forgotten once the first drumbeats were heard. The Rifles was a very good marching battalion. In barracks the Rifles' pace of 140 paces to the minute, sometimes more, was rigidly observed but marching outside was slower and more economical in energy. The writer learned all the dodges employed by the foot soldier - tricks like nicking the tops of the boots all round so that the leather did not cut into the flesh near the ankle; turning the socks inside out before a long march and rubbing wool with a piece of soap, then putting the socks back on in the usual way. After a few miles the sweat on the feet formed a nice squishy lather inside the boot and blisters were avoided. One pair of boots was brush polished and not burned or boned, and used for ceremonial parades and the other treated with dubbin, for field exercises.

Experimental equipment was issued to some of the rifle companies for testing. One particular item consisted of a thick canvas 'assault jerkin' which looked like a waistcoat, secured by straps or toggles, with large pockets for Bren gun magazines, ball ammunition and grenades. This was not considered practicable and the whole batch was returned. Every man was also issued with a thick toggle rope with a loop at one end, about six feet long. Threaded together the ropes were thought useful for crossing narrow rivers or, fixed to an entrenching tool, hurled over a wall or rooftop, to facilitate climbing over these obstacles. The toggle ropes did not survive long and were gradually discarded before the battalion went into action.

1944. The battalion, then part of the 6th Airborne Division, took part in the glider landing east of the River Orne on D-Day (June 6th). For months the men carried out the tasks for which they had been carefully prepared for so long. Marching, digging, patrolling and fighting, the days turned into weeks, then months before they reached the Seine at the end of August.

Returning to the United Kingdom the battalion resumed its pattern of training as before and, with a brief excursion to Europe to take part in the Ardennes campaign at Christmas the battalion prepared for its final operation.

1945. On March 24th ('Operation Varsity') the battalion landed at Hamminkeln east of the Rhine, again by Horsa gliders. On the drive to the Baltic coast it was a question of hard marching throughout but a new situation arose as the pace of the Allied offensive quickened. The retreating German army abandoned vast stores of equipment and transport. First of all the writer had the opportunity of trying on brand new leather and felt winter boots meant for German soldiers on the Eastern front but never issued to them. These were far too heavy and hot for marching in a European spring so were soon discarded. A large consignment of Italian army socks was seized and distributed amongst the battalion. These, too, were soon thrown away as they were made of cheap cotton and wool and cut the feet dreadfully. The division soon became more mobile as some rode on the tops of Churchill and Sherman tanks - a most uncomfortable experience for some as the hot exhausts scorched the soles of the boots of those standing nearby - and other acquired forms of transport. The writer, with the assistance of a lance-corporal of mechanical bent, 'rescued' a German half-tracked armoured personnel carrier which had been abandoned, upside down, in a sandpit. With this vehicle it was possible to by-pass the long lines of marching infantry, guns, tanks and other mechanical transport on the choked roads by breaking through the hedgerows and swanning across open land until there was a gap in the traffic, allowing us to resume our route towards the Baltic coast. Eventually because of the drain on petrol supplies men of the 6th Airborne Division were ordered to abandon their personnel carriers, motor cars, command vehicles and a weird assortment of other mechanical transport seized from the enemy and, once again, resumed their advance on foot.

Just before the Baltic coast was reached and junction with the Soviet Army established there were a number of rivers to be crossed. Some had to be negotiated by scrambling over the wrecked girders of bridges all but destroyed by the retreating Reichswehr. After each crossing, there being no time to take off and drain the boots of water, the marching had to go on. Once again there was the not uncomfortable sensation and sound of wet socks and feet squelching around inside the boots. Eventually the warmth dried the wool of the socks and feet and, miraculously, no blisters resulted. By this time of the war the average infantryman's soles had become hard and leathery and no amount of damp percolating the boot leather seemed to do any lasting harm to footwear or feet.

In the last few weeks before the actual end of hostilities the scenes on the roads were nearly beyond belief. Facing the advancing British infantry and armour were columns of German civilians, with horses, prams and carts, fleeing from the Russians, Soviet former prisoners-of-war, some armed with captured weapons, terrorising the local inhabitants and, most amazing of all, thousands of German troops, nearly all armed to the teeth, some with their regimental bands, marching south, en route to prisoner-of-war camps. Their horse-drawn transport rumbled past, with, in some cases, German officers being driven in the military Volkswagens (military jeeps). One of these vehicles was stopped by the writer and a couple of his comrades, and the occupants, much against their will, ordered to dismount and travel to captivity on foot. The vehicle was then loaded with ammunition and joined in the advance.

A month or so after the war with Germany had terminated, the writer's battalion returned home and, after replacing the not inconsiderable losses of men and equipment in action, was sent on embarkation leave.

As the war against Japan continued it was decided by the powers-that-be that three airborne divisions, one American and the 1st and 6th British Airborne, would be dropped on the line of retreat then being taken by the Japanese Army in Burma. With this in mind the men of the battalion were issued with new equipment, in the form of the new No.5 ('Jungle') rifle, shorter and lighter in weight than the No.4 previously issued. Light 1945 pattern equipment, jungle-green vests and underpants, rot-proof socks, green towels and so on were also provided for use in the new theatre of war.

Fortunately, hostilities against Japan came to an end in August. For a time the battalion did not participate in any lengthy marches and it was then that an issue of foot and body powder reached the troops. Instructions of the tins read:

> Apply the powder freely after washing to feet and
> body, particularly in between the toes, in the groins
> [sic] and in the armpits.

As the battalion had been reinforced and re-equipped it was then ready for re-deployment and in November it sailed for Palestine with the rest of the 6th Airborne Division for internal security duties.

Later, the writer was appointed Regimental Sergeant major of the newly constituted divisional Training Centre. Part of the philosophy behind the setting up of the Centre was to re-introduce peacetime standards of discipline and drill as, during the war years, of necessity, these had been discarded as of little relevance in the front-line situation. As a result, in the hot sunshine, on blindingly white parade grounds, NCOs of the Division were put through the routine of practising drill instruction techniques in readiness for the new intake joining the various battalions.

1947. After his demobilisation from the Army the writer rejoined the Portsmouth City Police in March. Since that time he has kept up the programme, learned many years ago, of road walking and running (now called 'jogging' by the aficionados, wearing training shoes instead of army boots).

1961. For a wager the writer walked around the coast of the Isle of Wight (approximately 62 miles - 99.2km) in 23 hours 35 minutes. This march was a continuous affair but for five minutes break at each clock hour for refreshment. Every five miles or so the socks were changed - from foot to foot, then inside out, then a complete change to a fresh pair and so on. As a result, when the journey was completed, there were no blisters or other signs of damage to the feet. A 20lb load was carried in a rucksack - of water, food, maps, groundsheet and stationery. The boots worn were one of a pair issued for the cancelled operation in Burma in 1945 - of an Australian pattern, brown in colour, with sewn-in tongues.

1990. By courtesy of the Army authorities the writer visited the Guards Training Depot at Pirbright, Surrey. He witnessed a number of squads of Foot Guards being drilled on the square. He is pleased to report that the standards of marching and drill and the expertise of the drill instructors there are as high as he experienced at Chelsea Barracks so many years ago.

BIBLIOGRAPHY AND SOURCES

Abstract of the Field Exercise and Evolutions of the Army. (By His Majesty's Command printed by W.Clowes, 1824)

ANDERSON, Charles R. *The Grunts.* (Novato, California, 1983)

ATKINSON, C.T. *The Royal Hampshire Regiment.* (Robert Maclehose, 1950)

ATKINSON, Captain G.F. *The Campaign in India, 1857-58.* (1859)

BAKER, Mark. *NAM.* (Abacus, 1982)

BARBUSSE, Henri. *Le feu.* (Paris, 1917)

BARNES, Major R.M. *A History of the Regiments and Uniforms of the British Army.* (Seeley Service and Co, 1950)

BARNETT, Corelli. *Marlborough.* (Eyre Methuen, 1974)

BECKER, Peter. *Rule of Fear: Life and Times of Dingane, King of the Zulu.* (Longmans, 1964.)

Black and White Budget Magazine. (Black and White Publishing Co. 1900)

BLOND, G. (ed. R. Laffont) *La Grande Armée.* (1979)

BODIN, J.L. *Histoire de l'Infanterie Française.* (Paris)

BROPHY, John and PARTRIDGE, Eric. *The Long Trail: What the British Soldier sang and said in the Great War, 1914-1918.* (Andre Deutsch, 1965)

CARMICHAEL, Pat. *Mountain Battery.* (Devin Books, 1983)

CASSIN-SCOTT, Jack and FABB, John. *Military Bands and their Uniforms.* (Blandford Press)

CAVE, Colonel T. Sturmy. *History of the 1st Volunteer Battalion Hampshire Regiment, 1859-1889.* (Simpkin and Co. Ltd. n.d.)

Chilean Army Drill Manual. (extracts, translation)

CLEMENTS, Paul. *Marc Isambard Brunel.* (Longmans, 1970)

COBBETT, William. *The Progress of a Ploughboy to a Seat in Parliament.* (ed. William Reitzel, 1933)

CONNOLLY, Peter. *The Greek Armies.* (Macdonald Educational Books, 1977)

COOPER, K.W. *Little Men.* (Robert Hale, 1973)

CRUICKSHANK, C.G. *Elizabeth's Army.* (Oxford University Press, 1966)

CUNLIFFE, F.H.E. *The History of the Boer War.* Vol.1. (Methuen and Co. 1901)

Danish Army Drill Manual. (extracts, translation)

DEIGHTON, Len. *Blitzkrieg.* (Triad Panther, 1981)

DOUGLAS, R.B. ed. *From Valmy to Waterloo: Extracts from the Diary of Captain Charles François.* (London, 1910)

Drill (All Arms). (H.M.S.O. 1967)

Drill and Ceremonies. (Headquarters Department of the Army, Pentagon, Washington DC, 1986)

Drill Manual. (US Naval Academy, Annapolis, Maryland, 1976)

DUFFY, Christopher. *The Army of Mary Theresa: The Armed Forces of Imperial Austria, 1740-1780.* (David and Charles, 1977)

DUNLOP, Colonel J.K. *The Territorial Army Today.* (A & C Black, 1939)

EDGERTON, Robert B. *Like Lions they Fought: The Last Zulu War.* (Weidenfield and Nicolson, 1988)

EDMONDES, Sir Clement. *The Maner of our Moderne Training.* (1600)

ELLIS, John. *The Sharp End of War.* (Corgi, 1982)

ELTON, Lieutenant Colonel Richard. *The Compleat Body of the Art Military.* (1659)

Exerzier-Reglement fur die Infanterie. (Infantry regulations, Berlin, 1906)

Falklands Aftermath. (Marshall Cavendish Books Ltd, 1984)

FEATHERSTONE, Donald. *Weapons and Equipment of the Victorian Soldier.* (Blandford Press, 1978)

Field Exercise and Evolutions of the Army. (By His Majesty's Command - printed by W. Clowes, 1833)

Field Exercise and Evolutions of Infantry. (H.M.S.O. 1877)

Field Service Pocket Book. (H.M.S.O. 1914)

FIRTH, C.H. *Cromwell's Army.* (Methuen, 1902)

Formaldienstordnung ZDv 3/2. (Bundeswehr drill manual, 1987)

FORESTIER, Amédée. *The Roman Soldier.* (A & C Black, 1928)

FULLER, J.F.C. *Decisive Battles of the Western World.* (Eyre and Spottiswood, 1965)

FURSE, Colonel G.A. *The Art of Marching*. (W. Clowes, 1901)

GRANT, Michael. *The Army of the Caesars*. (Weidenfield and Nicolson, 1974)

GREEN, David. *Blenheim*. (Collins, 1974)

HASTINGS, Max and JENKINS, Simon. *The Battle for the Falklands*. (London, 1983)

Heeresdienstvorschrift 100/100: Führung im Gefecht. (Command and Control in Battle Bundeswehr publication, 1973)

HIBBERT, Christopher. (ed). *A Soldier of the 71st*. (Leo Cooper, 1975)

Historical Record of the 89th (Princess Victoria's) Regiment. Gale and Polden, 1888)

HOLMES, Richard. *The Firing Line*. ((Jonathan Cape, 1985)

HUNT, Lieutenant Colonel J. Mouat F. *Records of the Infantry Militia Battalions of the County of Southampton, 1757-1894*. (Longmans Green and Co. 1894)

Infantry Drill. (H.M.S.O. 1896)

Infantry Training. (H.M.S.O. 1926)

Instruction Rationnelle (Fiches Nos. 1-5). (French Army drill cards)

Irish Army (Defence Forces) Drill Manual. (extracts)

KANE, Brigadier General Richard. *The Wars of William III and Queen Anne*. (1735)

KEEGAN, John. *The Face of Battle*. (Penguin, 1978)

KEMP, Alan. *American Soldiers of the Revolution*. (Almark Publishing Company, USA, 1972)

KIPLING, Rudyard. *Barrack-room Ballads and other Verses*. (Methuen and Company, 1919)

KOCH, H.W. *History of Warfare*. (W.H. Smith and Bison Books, 1987)

KRIGE, Eileen Jensen. *The Social System of the Zulus*. (Shuter and Shooter. Pietermaritzburg, 1950)

LACROIX, Paul. *Military and Religious Life in the Middle Ages and the Period of Renaissance*. (Bickers and Son, 1874)

LONGFORD, Elizabeth. *Wellington: The Years of the Sword*. (World Books, 1969)

LUNT, James. *From Sepoy to Subedar*. (Routledge and Paul, 1970)

McGOWAN, Robert and HANDS, Jeremy. *Don't cry for me, Sergeant Major.*(Futura, 1988)

McGUFFIE, T.H. (ed) *Rank and File.* (Hutchinson, 1964)

MAJDALANY, Fred. *The Monastery.* (London, 1950)

Manual of Elementary Drill (All Arms). (H.M.S.O. 1935)

Mehterhane: Türkiye Turing Ve Otomobil Kurumi. (Turkish government publication with details of history of military bands)

Memoirs of Captain Liddell Hart. Vol.1 (Cassell, 1965)

MYATT, Frederick. *The Soldier's Trade.* (Macdonald and Jane's, 1974)

NEUBERG, Victor. *Gone for a Soldier.* (Cassell, 1989)

NEVILL, Ralph. *British Military Prints.* (Connoisseur Publishing Company, 1909)

Observer newspaper, June 17th 1990. (re: 6,000 mile march of infantry in the Peninsular War)

O'LOGHLEN, Lieutenant Terence, H.M. Marine Forces. *The Marine Volunteer: Exercise, Firings and Evolutions of Infantry.* (W. Griffin, 1766)

ONIONS, C.T. (ed). *Oxford Dictionary of English Etymology.* (Clarendon Press, 1966)

Oxfordshire Light Infantry and (43rd and 52nd) Chronicle, 1892, 1903, 1904 and 1905.

PARTRIDGE, Eric. *Origins: A Short Etymological Dictionary of Modern English.* (Routledge and Kegan Paul, 1958)

PHIPPS, Lieutenant J, 70th Regiment. *A System of Military Discipline for H.M. Army.* (J. Millan, 1777)

RASIN, J.A. *Art of War in the Feudal Period.* (Berlin, 1960)

RAY, Charles. (ed). *Everybody's Enquire Within.* (Amalgamated Press, London circa 1937)

ROBINSON, Commander Charles N. *Navy and Army Illustrated Magazine, Vol.3.* (Hudson and Kearns and George Newnes, 1896)

ROSEN, Erwin. *In the Foreign Legion.* (1910)

RUSSELL, John, Ensign and Adjutant 1st Battalion Royal Army of Reserve. *Instruction for Drill and Method of Performing the Eighteen Manoeuvres.* (C. Roworth, 1803)

SKEAT, Reverand Walter W. *Etymological Dictionary of the English Language*. (Clarendon Press, 1910)

SCOULLER, R.E. *The Armies of Queen Anne*. (Oxford University Press, 1966)

Soviet Army Drill Manual. (translated extracts)

Spanish Army Drill Manual. (translated extracts)

STALLINGS, Lawrence (ed). *The First World War*. (Daily Express Publications, 1933)

Standard Encyclopaedia of Southern Africa. (Nasou Limited, South Africa, 1970)

STRONG, Donald. *The Early Etruscans*. (Evans Brothers Limited, 1968)

SUTTON, John and WALKER, John. *From Horse to Helicopter*. (Leo Cooper, 1990)

Swiss Army Drill Manual. (translated extracts)

The Kiwi Story, 1905-1960. (Melbourne, Australia 1960)

The New Zealand Army 1840s to 1980s. (Army General Staff, Wellington, 1982)

TREBLE, H.A. and KING, K.M. *Everyday Life in Rome*. (Clarendon Press, 1930)

TUCKER, Colonel John Montmorency. *Life of the Duke of Wellington*. (James Blackwood, circa 1890)

Turkish Army Drill Manual. (translated extracts)

Visier magazine. (Militärverlag der DDR - Berlin, 1990)

WALROND, Colonel H. *Historical Records of the 1st Devon Militia*. (Longmans Green and Company, 1897)

WALTER, John. *Arms and Equipment of the British Army*. (Greenhill Books, 1866)

War in the Falklands. (*Sunday Express Magazine* team - Book Club Associates, 1982)

War Office Papers II M49/239. (Portsmouth Corps of Hampshire Volunteers sergeants' application for Light Dragoon carbines to replace pikes, 1804, 'as they are much laughed at by the populace and are unwilling to go out with them.'

WATTEVILLE, Colonel H. de. *The British Soldier*. (J.M. Dent and Sons, 1954)

WELLS, H.G. *The Outline of History*. (Waverley Book Company Ltd, 1925)

WESTMAN, Stephen. *Surgeon with the Kaiser's Army*. (London, 1968)

WHITING, Charles. *The Poor Bloody Infantry*. (Stanley Paul, 1987)

WILKINSON, Sir J. Gardner. *Manners and Customs of the Ancient Egyptians*. (John Murray, 1841)

WINSTOCK, Lewis. *Songs and Music of the Redcoats, 1642-1902*. (Leo Cooper, 1970)

WLADIMIRZOW, S. *Die Gesellschaftsordnung der Mongolen*. (Leningrad, 1934. Russian language edition re Mongol conquests)

WOOD, Walter. *The Romance of Regimental Marches*. (William Clowes, circa 1932)

WOOD, Walter. *British Regiments in War and Peace: The Northumberland Fusiliers*. (1901)

INDEX

Figures in italics refer to illustrations

Models of Egyptian bowmen from tomb of Mesehti circa 2000 BC.
Egyptian Museum, Cairo

Models of Egyptian spearmen from tomb of Mesehti circa 200 BC.
Egyptian Museum, Cairo

Warriors represented on a bronze *situla* found at Certosa near Bologna,
Italy, dating from 5th/6th centuries BC. *Museo Civico Archaelogico, Bologna*

Roman Legionaries of the 2nd century AD with loads. *R. Embleton*

Above: Pottery figures of warriors
from the Han Dynasty (206 BC -
220 AD).   *Xinhua News Agency*
Right: A Janissary soldier of the
14th century. The Janissaries
constituted the standing army of
the Ottoman Empire from 1330 to
1826.   *Keubke*
Below: A Roman drill-master by
Amédee Forestier. *A & C Black, 1928*

Right: An English army on the march 1581. The pike and harquebus were the most important weapons of the foot soldier at this time.

Below: A modern reproduction of the battle of Naseby during the English Civil War 1642. Royalist troops before the start of the 'battle.' *From a Weetabix commercial television advertisement - by kind permission of Messrs Howard-Spink*

Below right:: Prussian infantry loading their muskets before a battle (18th century) *DDR Army Museum, Dresden*

Top left: Prussian infantry engaged in platoon-firing (18th century). Whilst the second rank fire by platoons the front rank kneel, grounding the butts of their muskets in readiness for a charge of enemy cavalry.
DDR Army Museum, Dresden

Bottom left: Prussian infantry advancing in line. *Keubke*

Above: Painting 'The Thin Red Line', depicting an incident during the battle of Balaklava during the Crimean War (1854-55) when Scottish infantry repulsed a Russian cavalry attack. *Portsmouth City Museums and Art Gallery*

Below: 'Soldiers Drilling' by J.A. Atkinson, 1807. *British Museum*

Top: British Marines filling water-bottles on the march from Ostend,
August 1914. *Imperial War Museum*

Above: An outstanding example of the art of marching by a unit of British
troops of the First World War period. Their identity is unknown but they
probably belong to a Regular Army battalion, judging from their standard
of marching and their expertly rolled puttees.

Top right: 1st Battalion the South Staffordshire Regiment on a route
march at Aldershot in the 1930s. *Ron Harris*

Right: British troops having their feet inspected after a route march circa
1920. *Bernard Collins*

March-past of German troops at Nuremberg 1932.   *DDR Army Museum, Dresden*

March-past of the Condor Legion, German Army, in Berlin 1939.
DDR Army Museum, Dresden

Men of the Royal Scots Fusiliers on a training march, North Sea coast
1940.   *Imperial War Museum*

Soldiers of the German Wehrmacht on the march 1941.
DDR Army Museum, Dresden

A body of Welsh Guards on a training march in Italy 1944.
Imperial War Museum
British parachutists after landing at Arnhem 1944 using airborne
handcarts for equipment and commandeered bicycles.
Airborne Forces Museum

Colour Guard of Netherlands Jagers Regiment 1948.
Military History Section Netherlands Army Staff
Australian soldiers in summer ceremonial parade uniform, marching past
in slow-time.   *Australian Army Public Relations*

March-past of DDR People's Army (East Germany) 1957.   *Keubke*

Top: Burmese Army march-past

Above: A contingent of the Chinese People's Liberation Army (Naval Force) using the parade step.   *Xinhua News Agency*

Close-up of Chilean
soldier using the parade
step.
Chilean Government

Troops of the Chinese
Republic (Taiwan) on
parade. *Chinese Republic
Government*

Finnish soldiers on parade.   *Army General Headquarters*

A company of the West German Bundeswehr on parade.
West German Defence Ministry

Top left: Military parade of the
Czechoslovak People's Army.
Czechoslovak People's Army

Top: Irish Army - the brisk marching
style is similar to that of the British
Army.   *Irish Defence Forces*

Left: Ghanaian infantry marching
past.   *Ghanaian Government*

Greek infantry in fighting order. Note the arms swung over shoulder
height.   *Greek Government*

Indonesian Armed Forces during a march-past.

Guards recruits on the march. (Note how arms are forced back to their fullest extent)   *R.D. Ostler*

Italian Grenadiers marching past.   *Italian Ministry of Defence*

Hungarian troops using the parade step.

Hungarian Government Foreign Affairs Department

Hungarian troops in summer uniform using the parade step.
Hungarian Government Foreign Affairs Department

Italian Bersaglieri wearing their distinctive headdress and using the traditional march at the double.   *Italian Ministry of Defence*

Jordanian armed forces march-past. *Jordanian Government*
Japanese airborne troops. *Japan Defense Agency*

Above: Nicaraguan Army using the parade step.
Left: Detachment of the 1st Mechanised Infantry Division of the Polish Army.
Below: Band of the Norwegian King's Guard.
Headquarters Defence Command Norway

Opposite page, top left: A soldier of the Romanian Army demonstrating the parade step.   *Romanian Government*

Top right: Sailors of the Soviet Navy and Royal Navy at the Royal Navy Memorial, Portsmouth 1990. Note the similar positions of 'Attention'. *'News' Portsmouth*

Below: Spanish infantry in summer uniform.   *Spanish Ministry of Defence DRISDE*

This page, above: A detachment of 32 Battalion South African Infantry on parade in Ovamboland, South-West Africa.   *South African Defence Force Public Relations*

Below: Spanish infantry marching past.   *Spanish Ministry of Defence DRISDE*

Left: A Soviet Army parade in Red Square, Moscow.   *USSR Goskomizdat*

Below: A Soviet Army regimental band marching 'at ease' near Red Square.

Below left: Scottish recruits marching in Slow Time during a platoon passing-out parade at Scottish Division Depot 1988.

Scottish Division Depot and D.C. Murray

Above: NCOs of 1st Battalion The Royal Irish Rangers Drum Platoon.

Royal Irish Rangers Depot

Infantry of the United States Army on parade at Fort Benning, Georgia.
US Army photograph by Marilyn Balzarini

Yugoslav infantry on a route march.   *Yugoslav Secretariat for National Defence*

A detachment of the 1st Battalion The Royal Irish Rangers on public duties at Buckingham Palace. *Royal Irish Rangers Depot*

Above: A unit of the Yugoslav People's Army using the parade step.
Yugoslav Secretariat for National Defence
Below: Detail from a painting of 'Ommeganck (or Procession) of Brussels,
31st May 1615', by Denis Van Alsloot. Note the drum and flute players and
the men firing harquebuses with and without forked rests, all, apparently,
in step with the music. *Victoria and Albert Museum*

Top left: A Fusilier of the Royal Welsh Fusiliers standing at Attention with a SA80 rifle.   *Prince of Wales's Division Depot*

Right: A sergeant of the Royal Welsh Fusiliers of the Waterloo period on the Wellington Monument near Hyde Park, London. *Keubke*

Below: Troopers of cavalry in the Imperial German Army being taught the rudiments of marching, possibly the parade (or 'goose') step circa 1900. *Keubke*

Left: German infantry singing on the march, 1940. *DDR Army Museum, Dresden*

Below: Soldiers of the DDR People's Army (East Germany) being taught the parade step 1978.

DDR Army Museum, Dresden

Top right: Pipes and drums of the 1st Battalion The Queen's Own Highlanders.

Colour Sergeant K.W. Hunter 1/QOH

Below right: Infantry of the DDR People's Army (East Germany) singing on the march, 1964. *DDR Army Museum, Dresden*

Above: Ghanaian infantry on the march (a few are singing).
Ghana Government
Below: Recruits of the Chinese People's Liberation Army (Ground Force Unit) practising the parade step. (The bricks on their insteps are to strengthen the thigh muscles which are liable to overstrain when performing this strenuous step) *Xinhua News Agency*

Above: Troops aligning themselves before a march at Fort Benning, Georgia. This procedure is known as 'Covering' in the US Army and enables each man to observe his correct distance from the man in front (30 inches). *US Army photograph by Marilyn Balzarini*
Below: Drill Instructors of the 1st Battalion The Irish Guards marching with the pacestick. *1st Battalion Irish Guards*

Above left: Private of the 41st (Invalids) Regiment circa 1751. First used as a Marching Regiment in 1787 after years of garrison duties, it later became the Welch Regiment. *By permission of the Trustees of the Welch Regiment Museum of the Royal Regiment of Wales.*

Above right: A Private of The King's Own Regiment in tropical uniform, wearing full marching order circa 1897.

Right: A British Army Private soldier wearing full marching order during the First World War. Wearing this equipment, plus ammunition bandoliers, shovels, pickaxes, Lewis or Vickers machine-guns and, sometimes, heavy and unwieldy rolls of barbed wire, the infantry struggled across shell-torn No Man's Land, lashed by enemy fire, machine-gun, mortar and artillery fire in the disastrous First Battle of the Somme in 1916. *Imperial War Museum*

Australian infantry on field exercise, lightly camouflaged. *Australian Government*

Greek Ezvones in traditional uniform, demonstrating their unique style of marching. *Greek Government*

Indian infantry in fighting order.   *Indian Government*

Italian Grenadiers Regiment in ceremonial uniform.   *Italian Ministry of Defence*

Italian Alpini infantry.   *Italian Ministry of Defence*

Norwegian infantry on exercise, lightly camouflaged.
Headquarters Defence Command, Norway

Top left: A soldier of a British Parachute Battalion in 1990 camouflaged uniform and equipment.
Ministry of Defence Crown Copyright
Top right: A soldier of the Swiss Army in fighting order.
Swiss Government
Left: A soldier of the Special Air Service Regiment (SAS) circa 1970 engaged in endurance training, wearing full marching order.
SAS Regiment

Above: A unit of Soviet Special Forces (Spetznaz) on manoeuvres.
USSR Goskomizdat
Left: Legionnaires of the French Foreign Legion singing on the march.
Top right: A soldier of the Swedish Army wearing camouflaged uniform.
Swedish Ministry of Defence Information Section
Right: The 52nd Light Infantry on the record-breaking forced march to Talavera in 1809 during the Peninsular War. *Royal Green Jackets Regiment HQ*

Above: US Military Academy, West Point - June Week Parade - Cadets
wearing traditional ceremonial uniform 1979.   *US Army*
Below: 3rd Battalion of the King's Royal Rifle Corps on the march during
the Zulu War of 1879.   *Royal Green Jackets Regiment HQ*

Top: 2nd Battalion 60th Rifles on the Kabul to Kandahar march, 1880.
Royal Green Jackets Regiment HQ
Middle: 1st Battalion the King's Royal Rifle Corps at the end of the retreat
from Dundee, South Africa, during the Boer War 1899.   *Royal Green
Jackets Regiment HQ*
Above: Royal Navy field-gunners, training for the Royal Tournament Field
Gun Competition, clad in uniforms of the period re-enact the famous
march of the Naval Brigade from HMS Powerful, a distance of 189 miles.
With their heavy guns they played an important part in the relief of
Ladysmith in the Boer War.   *'News', Portsmouth*

Troops of the 1st Battalion The Connaught Rangers on the march in the desert in Mesopotamia during the First World War.   *Imperial War Museum*

1st Battalion King's Royal Rifle Corps on the march from Rawalpindi to Razmak, a distance of over 240 miles in twenty days, 1926.
Royal Green Jackets Regiment HQ

Chinese Red Army soldiers at the base area in Northern Shensi province
after the famous 'Long March' 1934/35.   *Xinhua News Agency*

Australian infantry on an endurance march.   *Australian Government*

Top left: Canadian troops on a tactical march.
Canadian Government
Top right: Israeli infantry on an endurance march.
Israeli Government
Left: A marching unit of the Czechoslovak People's Army during a field exercise 1984.
Czechoslovak People's Army

A detachment of the Netherlands Corps of National Reserve on a four-day
march at Nijmegen, 1985   *Military History Section Netherlands Army Staff*

Recruits of the South African Army on basic training undergoing an
endurance route march.   *South African Defence Force Public Relations*

A unit of Royal Marine Commandos on endurance training, carrying
maximum loads.   *Royal Marine Commando Training Centre*

Guardsmen of the 1st Battalion The Irish Guards on an endurance
training exercise.   *1st Battalion Irish Guards*

Recruits from Scottish Division Depot on a forced march.
Scottish Division Depot and D.C. Murray

2nd Battalion The Royal Irish Rangers on manoeuvres over an old
battlefield of the Falklands War of 1982. *2nd Royal Irish Rangers*

A jungle patrol of 1st Battalion The Royal Ulster Rifles in Sarawak.
Royal Ulster Rifles Association

A detachment of the Women's American Army Corps on a forced march.
US Department of the Army

Above: Soldier of the 2nd Battalion The Royal Irish Rangers on exercise in the Falklands. *2nd Bn. Royal Irish Rangers*

Opposite page, top: Soldiers of the 1st Battalion The Hampshire Regiment on patrol in Northern Ireland 1987. *1st Battalion Hampshire Regiment*

Left: Soldiers of the 1st Battalion The Parachute Regiment on a forced march. *1st Battalion Parachute Regiment*

Right: A soldier of the 1st Battalion The Royal Irish Rangers, in fighting order, carrying a heavy machine-gun during manoeuvres.

1st Battalion Royal Irish Rangers

The Grand Elector of Brandenberg crossing the Kurisches Haff to fight against the Swedes in 1679. Kurfurst Fredrich Wilhelm von Brandenburg is standing up in the sleigh. *Keubke*

Troops of the Northamptonshire Regiment boarding a Vickers Victoria at Heliopolis, Egypt, bound for Iraq in 1932. Note 1908 pattern equipment, 'squared off' packs, khaki drill uniforms with hosetops and puttees. *RAF Brize Norton*

Men of the 6th Airborne Division loading folding bicycles into a Horsa glider before the D-Day airborne assault on Normandy, June 1944.
Airborne Forces Museum

Men of a battalion of Royal Northumberland Fusiliers being carried by a Centurion tank of the King's Royal Irish Hussars up a bank of the Imjin river on return from a patrol during the Korean War (1950-53).
Courtesy of Leo Cooper, publisher

Troops of the Chinese People's Liberation Army in armoured personnel
carriers in 1986. *Xinhua News Agency*

South African Army APC 'Buffel'. *Krygkor Armscor, Pretoria*

Six-wheeler armoured personnel carrier 'Ratel 90' of the South African Army. *Krygkor Armscor, Pretoria*

A section of the 1st Battalion The Royal Irish Rangers dismounting from an armoured personnel carrier. *1st Battalion Royal Irish Rangers*

GKN Warrior APC in action with infantry. *GKN Defence*

British soldiers of the 3rd Battalion Royal Regiment of Fusiliers, marching in full battledress with tank escort as the countdown to the Gulf Conflict continued. *Rex Features*